Seven keys to Baldpate

A mysterious melodramatic farce, in a prologue, two acts, and an epilogue

George M. Cohan

Alpha Editions

This edition published in 2019

ISBN : 9789353866075

Design and Setting By
Alpha Editions
email - alphaedis@gmail.com

As per information held with us this book is in Public Domain.
This book is a reproduction of an important historical work.
Alpha Editions uses the best technology to reproduce historical
work in the same manner it was first published to preserve its
original nature. Any marks or number seen are left intentionally
to preserve its true form.

Seven Keys To Baldpate

A MYSTERIOUS MELODRAMATIC FARCE

In a Prologue, Two Acts and an Epilogue

BY

GEORGE M. COHAN

Based on the Novel, "Seven Keys to Baldpate," by Earl Derr Biggers, published and duly copyrighted by The Bobbs-Merrill Company, 1913

DULY COPYRIGHTED, 1913, 1914, IN THE UNITED STATES OF AMERICA, THE DOMINION OF CANADA, GREAT BRITAIN, AUSTRALIA AND BY INTERNATIONAL COPYRIGHT, BY GEORGE M. COHAN

All Rights Reserved

CAUTION: Professionals and amateurs are hereby warned that "SEVEN KEYS TO BALDPATE," being fully protected under the copyright laws of the United States of America, Great Britain, the Dominion of Canada, and other countries of the world, is subject to a royalty, and anyone presenting the play without the consent of the author or his authorized agents will be liable to the penalties by law provided. Applications for the amateur acting rights must be made to SAMUEL FRENCH, 25 West 45th Street, New York, N. Y.

NEW YORK	LONDON
SAMUEL FRENCH	SAMUEL FRENCH, LTD.
PUBLISHER	26 SOUTHAMPTON STREET
25 WEST 45TH STREET	STRAND

Based on the Novel, "Seven Keys to Baldpate," by Earl Derr Biggers, published and duly copyrighted by The Bobbs-Merrill Company, 1913

DULY COPYRIGHTED, 1913, 1914, IN THE UNITED STATES OF AMERICA, THE DOMINION OF CANADA, GREAT BRITAIN, AUSTRALIA AND BY INTERNATIONAL COPYRIGHT, BY GEORGE M. COHAN

All Rights Reserved

"Seven Keys to Baldpate"

Especial notice should be taken that the possession of this book without a valid contract for production first having been obtained from the publisher, confers no right or license to professionals or amateurs to produce the play publicly or in private for gain or charity.

In its present form this play is dedicated to the reading public only, and no performance, representation, production, recitation, public reading or radio broadcasting may be given except by special arrangement with Samuel French, 25 West 45th Street, New York.

Amateur royalty quoted on application.

Whenever the play is produced by amateurs the following notice must appear on all programs, printing and advertising for the play: "Produced by special arrangement with Samuel French of New York."

Attention is called to the penalty provided by law for any infringement of the author's rights, as follows.

"SECTION 4966:—Any person publicly performing or representing any dramatic or musical composition for which copyright has been obtained, without the consent of the proprietor of said dramatic or musical composition, or his heirs and assigns, shall be liable for damages thereof, such damages, in all cases to be assessed at such sum, not less than one hundred dollars for the first and fifty dollars for every subsequent performance, as to the court shall appear to be just. If the unlawful performance and representation be wilful and for profit, such person or persons shall be guilty of a misdemeanor, and upon conviction shall be imprisoned for a period not exceeding one year."—U. S. Revised Statutes: Title 60, Chap. 3.

The following is a copy of the playbill of the first performance of "SEVEN KEYS TO BALDPATE," as produced at the Astor Theatre, New York, September 22nd, 1913.

COHAN & HARRIS

Present

SEVEN KEYS TO BALDPATE

A Melodramatic Farce
in
A Prologue, Two Acts, and An Epilogue

BY
GEORGE M. COHAN

Based on the Novel, "Seven Keys to Baldpate," by Earl Derr Biggers, published by the Bobbs-Merrill Company.

THE CAST
(In the order of their appearance)

ELIJAH QUIMBY	*Edgar Halstead*
MRS. QUIMBY	*Jessie Grahame*
WILLIAM HALLOWELL MAGEE	*Wallace Eddinger*
JOHN BLAND	*Purnell B. Pratt*
MARY NORTON	*Margaret Greene*
MRS. RHODES	*Lorena Atwood*
PETERS, the hermit	*Joseph Allen*
MYRA THORNHILL	*Gail Kane*
LOU MAX	*Roy Fairchild*
JIM CARGAN	*Martin Alsop*
THOMAS HAYDEN	*Claude Brooke*
JIGGS KENNEDY	*Carleton Macy*
THE OWNER OF BALDPATE	*John C. King*

The scene is laid in the office of Baldpate Inn.
TIME: *The Present.*

CHARACTERS

(In the order of their appearance)

ELIJAH QUIMBY, *the caretaker of Baldpate Inn.*
MRS. QUIMBY, *the caretaker's wife.*
WILLIAM HALLOWELL MAGEE, *the novelist.*
JOHN BLAND, *the millionaire's right hand man.*
MARY NORTON, *the newspaper reporter.*
MRS. RHODES, *the charming widow.*
PETERS, *the Hermit of Baldpate.*
MYRA THORNHILL, *the blackmailer.*
LOU MAX, *the Mayor's man "Friday."*
JIM CARGAN, *the crooked mayor of Reuton.*
THOMAS HAYDEN, *the president of the R. and E. Suburban R.R.*
JIGGS KENNEDY, *Chief of Police of Asquewan Falls.*
THE OWNER OF BALDPATE.

The scene is laid in the office of Baldpate Inn.
Time: The Present.

Produced for the first time on any stage at Parsons' Theatre, Hartford, Conn., September 15, 1913.
Opened at the Astor Theatre, New York City, September 22, 1913.
Written, staged and produced by GEO. M. COHAN.
No. Two Company opened at COHAN'S *Grand Opera House, Chicago, February 15, 1914.*

SEVEN KEYS TO BALDPATE

ACT I

Scene explained on diagram later.

At Rise *of curtain the stage is bare. No lights on the stage except the rays of the moon shining through glass door and the sky above. The wind is heard howling outside. The effect is that of a terrific storm taking place. Everything within the scene proves that it is a deserted, desolate spot; in fact, an inn, a summer resort on the mountains closed for the winter.*

After thirty seconds Elijah Quimby *appears at glass door upstage and is seen swinging a lantern. He does this as if guiding someone who is following; a sort of signal to* Mrs. Quimby, *who presently appears trudging behind him. He hands her the lantern while he fumbles with a bunch of keys he has taken from his pocket. She gives him a light from the lantern while he finds the right key and unlocks the door. As the door swings open the wind is heard howling unmercifully. He holds the door open for her to enter, then follows her in, closing the door. They both stamp their feet to get them warm.* Mrs. Quimby *goes down* R.C., *holding up lantern and*

6 SEVEN KEYS TO BALDPATE

peering around room, then goes up R. *and to* C. *and down to table* L., *on which she places the lantern.* QUIMBY, *after locking the door, goes slowly down* L. *to table, meanwhile stamping feet, removing ear-muffs and placing cap and mittens on table.* MRS. QUIMBY *removes her mittens, and they both stand rubbing their hands and ears. All this business is done without a word being spoken. The reason for it is to prove to the audience that the night is bitterly cold and that the two people are half frozen after their climb up the mountain.*

[margin note: "calls her"]

QUIMBY. (*At table* L., *right of* MRS. QUIMBY, *shivering*) You know, Mother, I think it's colder in here than it is outside.

MRS. QUIMBY. (*Shivering*) I was going to say the same thing, Elijah.

QUIMBY. Maybe we'd better open the door and let in some warm air.

[margin note: "rejects practical directing"]

MRS. QUIMBY. You'd better not; the snow'll blow all over the place. See if there's any logs over there and we'll build a fire. (*Indicates fireplace with a nod of her head.*)

QUIMBY. (*Starts* R., *stops and stamps his feet*) You know, Mother, I think my feet are froze. I can't feel 'em when I walk. (*Knocks hands together.*)

(TOWN *Clock Ready.*)

MRS. QUIMBY. I don't wonder, after that climb up the mountain. Lord, I'll never forget this night! I'm about perished. (*She straightens chairs, etc., while* QUIMBY *is looking for logs.*) Any logs there?

QUIMBY. Yep, plenty of 'em. I got this thing all ready, anyway. I was goin' to build a fire when I was up here last week. I'll have 'em blazin' in a minute if I can find them darned matches. (*Searches through his pockets.*) I can swear I put a box of 'em in my pocket before I left the house! (*Finds them.*) Yep, here they are!

MRS. QUIMBY. You'd better light a lamp first, so's you can see what you're doin'.

QUIMBY. That's a good idea.

(*Clock in distance strikes eleven while he is scratching match and lighting lamp over fireplace* R. *Note.—Footlights up slightly when lamp is turned up.*)

MRS. QUIMBY. (*Standing at foot of stairs*) Eleven o'clock.

QUIMBY. Yep, that's what it is—eleven o'clock. (*Goes upstage and looks through glass door.*) That train's been in over twenty minutes already. I suppose it's the storm that delays him. 'Tain't over a ten-minute walk up the mountain from the depot. (*Comes down* R.C.)

MRS. QUIMBY. (*Goes to* R., *near desk*) Maybe the train's late on account of the storm.

QUIMBY. No; I heard it signal the crossing at Asquewan Junction a half hour ago. That feller'll be here before we know it. (*Hands her matches.*) Light the other lamp, will you, Mother, while I get at this fire?

(MRS. QUIMBY *takes matches and lights lamp up* L., *near stairway. He builds fire in fireplace. Both are busily engaged in fixing room, heating and lighting it during following conversation:*)

MRS. QUIMBY. Maybe we should have gone to the depot to meet him?

QUIMBY. (*Going* C.) No; we shouldn't have done nothin' of the kind. The telegram just said to come here and to open up the place and have it ready for him. Them's the instructions, and them's the only things I foller—is instructions. (*Starts toward* R.)

MRS. QUIMBY. (*Going* C.) But what do you suppose anybody wants to be doin' in a summer hotel on the top of a mountain in the dead of winter?

QUIMBY. Mother, you know I can't figger out nothin'. (*Goes up to door, peers out, then comes down to* MRS. QUIMBY.) If I could I'd 'a' been a multi-millionaire years ago, instead of an old fool caretaker. (*Goes nearer to* MRS. QUIMBY.) Dust up a bit there, will you, Mother, and make the place look a little respectable? (*Goes toward fireplace.*) She'll be goin' all right in a minute now.

MRS. QUIMBY. (*Dusting with cloth she has taken from foot of stairs*) What's his name again?

QUIMBY. Magee, I think the telegram says. (*Meets* MRS. QUIMBY *at* C.)

MRS. QUIMBY. Magee?

QUIMBY. Wait a minute, I'll make sure. (*Takes telegram from his pocket.*)

MRS. QUIMBY. (*Takes telegram from him and goes* L.) Give it to me; I want to read it myself. The whole thing's very mysterious to me. (*Goes to table and sits, reading by light of lantern.*)

QUIMBY. (*Goes toward* MRS. QUIMBY—*fire begins to blaze up*) Of course it's mysterious, but it's none of our business. Mr. Bentley is the owner of Baldpate Inn. If Mr. Bentley wants to permit some darn fool to come to this place to be froze to death by stale air and to be frightened to death by spooks, it's his concern and not ours. (*Turns and looks at fire, which is blazing.*) Ah, there she goes, she's blazing up fine. That'll warm it up a little. (*Goes* L.C. *to* MRS. QUIMBY *during next speech.*)

MRS. QUIMBY. (*Reading message slowly*) "My friend, William Hallowell Magee, will arrive in Asquewan Falls to-night on the ten-forty. He will occupy Baldpate Inn, so be prepared to receive him there, and turn the key over to him and do whatever

SEVEN KEYS TO BALDPATE 9

you can to make him comfortable. He has important work to do, and has chosen Baldpate for his workshop. Follow instructions. Ask no questions. Hal Bentley."

QUIMBY. *(Has been listening attentively)* Sounds like them Black Hand notes they send to rich men, don't it?

MRS. QUIMBY. I can't understand it for the life of me. *(Hands telegram back to* QUIMBY.)

QUIMBY. Mother!

MRS. QUIMBY. *(Over to* QUIMBY c.) Yes?

QUIMBY. (R. *of* c.) Maybe the feller's committed some crime and is comin' here to hide.

MRS. QUIMBY. Do you think so, Elijah?

QUIMBY. I don't know; I say—mebbe.

MRS. QUIMBY. Well, if that's so, why should Mr. Bentley be interested in such a man?

QUIMBY. *(Thinks)* I never thought of that. *(Thinks.)* Well, whatever it is, it's none of our business, and we mustn't mix in other people's affairs. *(Goes* R.)

MRS. QUIMBY. *(Thinks a moment, then comes down near* QUIMBY) Elijah!

QUIMBY. *(Looks up)* What?

MRS. QUIMBY. Do you think I'd better fix up one of them rooms?

QUIMBY. Sure; he'll have to have a place to sleep. Here—*(Gives her key)*—that opens the linen closet. You'd better fix up that first room to the left. *(Points to room on balcony* R.) That's the one Mr. Bentley always takes when he comes.

MRS. QUIMBY. *(As she goes toward stairs, taking lantern from table)* And you'd better put another log on the fire. (QUIMBY *goes toward fireplace.)* He'll probably be chilled to the bone by the time he climbs that mountain. Do you think he'll find his way alone? *(Goes upstairs during speech.)*

QUIMBY. Oh, he'll find his way all right. The

station agent will most likely direct him. *(Puts log on fire, which blazes up.)*

Mrs. Quimby. *(Going up the stairs)* Occupying a summer hotel in the dead of winter! It beats all what some people will do! *(Exits door L., leaving door open.)*

Quimby. *(Takes out his pipe and sits thinking near fire)* Humph! It's pretty darned mysterious, all right. *(Lights pipe and smokes.)* I'll be jiggered if I can figger it out.

(Mrs. Quimby *remains inside room four counts after cue, then comes from room carrying linen and bed coverings in her arms. She crosses balcony to room* R. *of balcony and exits, closing door.* Quimby *sits smoking and thinking.* Magee *appears at door upstage and peers through. He is carrying a suit and typewriter case. He puts them down and knocks on window.* Quimby *doesn't move at first, but sits listening, to make sure he has heard a sound.* Magee *repeats the knocking.* Quimby *shifts around in his chair, looks up toward the window, sees a form there, then gets up and sneaks along down stage until he gets to foot of stairs, then calls in suppressed tones to* Mrs. Quimby.)

Quimby. Mother, Mother! *(No answer from* Mrs. Quimby. *He runs half-way upstairs and calls a bit louder)* Mother!

Mrs. Quimby. *(Appears on balcony, peers over and sees* Quimby) Did you call me, Elijah?

Quimby. Hush! Don't talk so loud! *(Warns her to be quiet.)*

Mrs. Quimby. *(Lowering her voice)* What's the matter? *(They both listen for a second.* Magee's *third rap comes.)* Good Lord, what's that?

SEVEN KEYS TO BALDPATE

QUIMBY. *(On stairs)* It's him—he's here! *(He points to door upstage.)*
MRS. QUIMBY. Who?
QUIMBY. The telegram—I mean the man.
MRS. QUIMBY. *(Starts down the stairs)* Where?
QUIMBY. At the door.

(MAGEE *again raps impatiently.*)

MRS. QUIMBY. *(Urging* QUIMBY *down the stairs)* Why don't you let him in?
QUIMBY. *(Both come downstairs)* Do you think I'd better?
MRS. QUIMBY. Well, ain't that what the telegram said?
QUIMBY. Why, yes, of course, but——
MRS. QUIMBY. *(Shoving* QUIMBY *toward door)* You got your instructions. Go on and do as you're told.

(MAGEE *knocks again and rattles the door-knob.*)

QUIMBY. *(In a loud voice as he goes up toward door)* Yes, yes; jest a minute, jest a minute!

(As QUIMBY *goes up to door,* MRS. QUIMBY *comes down* L. QUIMBY *unlocks door and swings it open. The wind howls.* MAGEE, *carrying the two cases, enters and comes to* C. *and stands bowing, first to* MRS. QUIMBY *and then to* QUIMBY, *then drops the cases in the middle of the stage. Looks around the room for a moment, wild-eyed, then sees fire burning and goes over to it as fast as his half-frozen legs will allow him. He pulls chair in front of fire and sits warming himself.* QUIMBYS *stand* C., *watching him in amazement. As soon as* MAGEE *has entered* QUIMBY *has locked the door and come*

down R. *As* MAGEE *sits,* QUIMBY *goes to* MRS. QUIMBY *at* L.C.)

MRS. QUIMBY. *(Aside to* QUIMBY*)* The poor thing's half froze.

QUIMBY. *(Approaches* MAGEE, MRS. QUIMBY *following him to fireplace)* What's the matter, young fellow, are you cold?

MAGEE. *(Smiles a sickly smile, shakes his head, laughs half-heartedly, then replies)* Humph! Am I cold! I feel pretty rocky, but I've got to laugh at that one.

MRS. QUIMBY. *(Aside to* QUIMBY*)* Better give him a drink of whiskey.

QUIMBY. Yes, I guess so. *(Takes flask from his pocket and hands it to* MAGEE*)* Here, young fellow, try a little of this.

MAGEE. *(Looks up, sees flask, and grabs it)* Thanks! *(Takes a long drink.* QUIMBY *goes* C. *to* MRS. QUIMBY.*)*

MRS. QUIMBY. *(Aside to* QUIMBY*)* Do you suppose it's him?

QUIMBY. *(Aside)* How do I know?

MRS. QUIMBY. *(Aside)* Well, ask him and find out.

MAGEE. *(Offers flask to* QUIMBY*)* Thanks again, a thousand thanks.

QUIMBY. Oh, you just put that in your pocket; you might need it later on.

MAGEE. Thanks.

(MRS. QUIMBY *picks up cases from floor and takes them to table* L.)

QUIMBY. You're Mr. Magee, ain't you?
MAGEE. Right! What's left of me is still Magee. You expected me, of course.

SEVEN KEYS TO BALDPATE   13

QUIMBY. Oh, yes; we got Mr. Bentley's telegram all right. My name's Quimby.
MAGEE. So I surmised.
QUIMBY. This lady is my wife, Mrs. Quimby. *(Points to* MRS. QUIMBY, *who crosses to* MAGEE *at fireplace.)*
MAGEE. I thought as much. Delighted, Mrs. Quimby. *(Bows to* MRS. QUIMBY *without rising.)*
MRS. QUIMBY. Glad to meet you, Mr. Magee.
MAGEE. You'll pardon me for not rising, but really I'm terribly cold.
MRS. QUIMBY. *(Goes to* QUIMBY *during following speech)* That's all right. You sit there and get het up. We've been living here in the mountains so long we don't mind the cold as much as strangers do, but even we felt it to-night, didn't we, Elijah?
QUIMBY. That's right, Mother; this is an uncommon cold night.
MAGEE. *(Rises, removes overcoat, muffler and hat, and places them on chair)* That little trip from the railroad station to the top of the mountain has taught me to firmly believe everything Jack London ever wrote about and everything old Dr. Cook ever lied about. *(Crosses to* L.C., *looking at everything, very much interested, and rubbing his hands.)* So this is Baldpate, is it? Well, well, well!
MRS. QUIMBY. *(*R.C., *aside to* QUIMBY*)* Don't he talk funny?
QUIMBY. *(*L. *of* MRS. QUIMBY—*aside)* Yes. Acts funny, too. Something's the matter with him, sure. *(Both watch* MAGEE *closely.)*
MAGEE. *(Coming* C.*)* You say you received Mr. Bentley's telegram saying I would be here?
QUIMBY. Yes; it only came about an hour ago, so we didn't have much time to prepare.
MAGEE. I didn't decide to come here until four o'clock this afternoon.

Mrs. Quimby. We was scared most to death gettin' a telegram in the middle of the night.

Magee. I'm very sorry to have taken you out on a night like this, but it was altogether necessary in order that I accomplish what I've set out to do. Let me see—the rooms above are equipped with fireplaces, I believe? *(Looks up at rooms on balcony.)*

Mrs. Quimby. *(Crosses C. to Magee)* Yes; I'm just fixin' up one of the rooms. I'll start the fire, too. I'll have it all ready for you inside of five minutes. *(Crosses to R., gets wood from box, and comes to R. of Quimby.)*

(LIGHTS Ready.)

Magee. I wish you would. *(Looks around room.)* Yes; this would be too big a barn to work in. *(Quimbys look at each other.)* I'll no doubt be more comfortable up there. *(Continues to take in surroundings.)*

Quimby. *(Aside to Mrs. Quimby)* He says he's goin' to work. I wonder what he means.

Mrs. Quimby. *(Aside, crossing to L. of Quimby)* Pump him. Try to find out. *(Aloud)* Give me the matches.

Quimby. Here you are. *(He hands her a box of matches. Mrs. Quimby, with wood in her arms, starts for stairs and goes up on balcony.)*

Magee. This, I presume, is the hotel office.

Quimby. That's right.

Magee. *(Strolls around stage looking at everything carefully. Quimby watching him closely)* Well, well! This certainly is old John H. Seclusion himself.

(Lights go up.)

Mr. *and* Mrs. Quimby. *(Together)* Good Lord, where did those lights come from? Good Lord, what's happened? *(As lights go up, Quimby darts*

behind desk R. MRS. QUIMBY *is leaning over balcony* C. *Both are frightened.)*
MAGEE. *(Laughs)* Don't be alarmed, Mrs. Quimby; it's all right. I think I can explain this thing. Mr. Bentley has probably had the power turned on. He knew I'd have to have some real light for this kind of work. (MRS. QUIMBY *exits into room* R. *on balcony, closing the door.* MAGEE *goes to* QUIMBY *up* R.) I suppose you're wondering what the devil I'm doing here.
QUIMBY. That's just what I was wondering, young fellow.
MAGEE. Well, I'll try to explain, although I'm not sure you'll understand. Sit down, Mr. Quimby. (QUIMBY *hesitates.)* It's all right, sit down. (QUIMBY *gets chair and places it* R.C., *then sits.)* Now, you are not, I take it, the sort of man to follow closely the light and frivolous literature of the day.
QUIMBY. How's that?
MAGEE. You don't read the sort of novels that are sold by the pound in the department stores.
QUIMBY. Nope.
MAGEE. Well, I write those novels.
QUIMBY. The dickens you do!
MAGEE. Wild, thrilling tales for the tired business man's tired wife; shots in the night; chases after fortunes; Cupid busy with his arrows all over the place. It's good fun—I like to do it, and—there's money in it.
QUIMBY. You don't mean to tell me!
MAGEE. Oh, yes, considerable. Of course, they say I'm a cheap melodramatic ranter. They say my thinking process is a scream. Perhaps they're right. *(Moves chair out and sits* L.C.)
QUIMBY. Perhaps.
MAGEE. Did you ever read "The Scarlet Satchel"?
QUIMBY. Never.
MAGEE. That's one of mine.

QUIMBY. Is it?

MAGEE. I've come here to Baldpate to think; to get away from melodrama, if possible; to do a novel so fine and literary that Henry Cabot Lodge will come to me with tears in his eyes and beg me to join his bunch of self-made immortals. And I'm going to do all this right here in this inn, sitting on this mountain, looking down on this little old world as Jove looked down from Olympus. What do you think of that?

QUIMBY. *(Shakes his head, affecting an air of understanding)* Maybe it's all for the best.

MAGEE. Of late I've been running short of material. *(Rises, moves chair to R. of table and goes to* QUIMBY.*)* I've needed inspiration. A title gave me that—"The lonesomest spot on earth," suggested by my very dear friend and your employer, Mr. Hal Bentley. "What and where is the lonesomest spot on earth?" I asked. "A summer resort in winter," said he. He told me of Baldpate—dared me to come. I took the dare—and here I am.

QUIMBY. *(Rising and going to* MAGEE *at* C.*)* You mean you're goin' to write a book?

MAGEE. That's just exactly what I'm going to do. I'm going to novelize Baldpate. I'm here to get atmosphere.

QUIMBY. *(Laughs)* Lord, you'll get plenty of that, all right! When are you goin' to start in?

MAGEE. Just as soon as I absorb my surroundings and make a few mental notes. You see, I do most of my work in the dead of night. I find I concentrate more readily from midnight on. But I must have absolute solitude. The crackle of the fire, the roar of the wind, and the ticking of my watch will alone bear me company at Baldpate Inn. This all sounds very strange and weird to you, I suppose.

QUIMBY. How's that?

MAGEE. I say, you can't quite fathom me.

"Seven Keys to Baldpate"

KENNEDY: "Who are you?"
OWNER: "I'm the owner of Baldpate."
Left to Right: Lou Max, Peters, Magee, Bland, Owner of Baldpate, Kennedy, Mary Norton, Mrs. Rhodes, Cargan, Hayden.

QUIMBY. Well, you're here of your own accord, I take it.
MAGEE. My dear Mr. Quimby, I'm here on a bet.
QUIMBY. On a bet!
MAGEE. Exactly. I have here an explanation of the thing in Bentley's handwriting. *(Takes paper from his pocket.)* Do you care to look it over yourself, or would you rather I'd read it to you?
QUIMBY. Yes, go on and read it—I like to hear you talk. *(Sits* R.C.*)*
MAGEE. *(Smiles)* Ah, then my personality has wormed its way into your good graces.
QUIMBY. How's that?
MAGEE. I mean to say, I evidently appeal to you.
QUIMBY. Well, I don't know as you particularly appeal to me, but——
MAGEE. But what?
QUIMBY. *(Laughs, confused)* Oh, I guess I better not say it.
MAGEE. Come on, what's on your mind? Tell me.
QUIMBY. Well, to be honest with you, I can't figger out whether you're a smart man or a damn fool.
MAGEE. *(Laughs)* Would you believe it, my dear sir, I've been stalled between those two opinions of myself for years? My publishers say I'm a smart man; my critics call me a damn fool. However, that's neither here nor there. This—*(Indicating paper)*—will perhaps clear away the cloud of mystery to some extent. Oh, perhaps Mrs. Quimby would be interested enough to hear this also. Will you call her, please?
QUIMBY. Sure! *(Rises and calls)* Mother! Oh, Mother!
MRS. QUIMBY. *(Appears at door* R. *on balcony and comes to* C. *of it)* Yes, I'm all through. Everything's ready up here. *(Leans over balcony* C.*)*

18   SEVEN KEYS TO BALDPATE

You'd better come up, Mister, and see if it satisfies you before we go.

MAGEE. It's all right, Mrs. Quimby. I'll take your word for it that everything's all right.

QUIMBY. Come on down here, Mother; Mr. Magee wants to read something to you. *(Places chair for her* R.C., *next his own.)*

MRS. QUIMBY. Is that so? *(Starts downstairs.)* I started the fire, so I guess the room'll be comfortable enough to sleep in by the time you get ready to go to bed. *(Is downstairs by now.)*

QUIMBY. Sit down, Mother.

MRS. QUIMBY. What!

QUIMBY. Go on. See, I'm sittin'. (MRS. QUIMBY *goes toward* QUIMBY.) Mr. Magee's goin' to tell us why he's here.

MRS. QUIMBY. *(Sits* L. *of* QUIMBY) Is that so? Lord, I'd love to know!

MAGEE. I have just explained to your husband that I am an author. I do popular novels, and I'm here to write a story—a story of Baldpate Mountain, laid in this very hotel, perhaps in this identical room. I am to complete this task within twenty-four hours, starting at midnight to-night.

QUIMBY. Understand, Mother? He's goin' to write a book.

MRS. QUIMBY. *(To* MAGEE*)* Goin' to write a book in twenty-four hours!

MAGEE. That is the wager that has been made between Mr. Bentley and myself. He claimed it couldn't be done. I claimed it could. Five thousand dollars' worth of his sporting blood boiled, and he dug for his fountain pen and check book. I covered the bet, and we posted the checks at the Forty-fourth street club. He was to choose the godforsaken spot. *(Looks around room.)* He succeeded. I ran to my apartments, placed some manuscript paper, a dozen sandwiches and my slippers in a suit-

case, grabbed my faithful typewriting machine, just
made the train, and here you see me, ready to win
or lose the wager, as the case may be.
QUIMBY. What do you think of that, Mother?
MRS. QUIMBY. *(To* MAGEE) I never heard of
such a thing!
MAGEE. Here is a copy of the agreement, in which
you will notice your name is mentioned, Mr. Quimby. Listen. *(Reads)* "You are to leave New York
City on the four-fifty-five for Asquewan Falls, arriving at ten-forty, and go direct to Baldpate Inn,
a-top the Baldpate Mountain, where you will be met
by my caretaker, Mr. Elijah Quimby, who, after
making you comfortable, will turn over to you the
key to the inn, the only key in existence." *(To*
QUIMBY) Is that correct?
QUIMBY. It's the only key I know of.
MRS. QUIMBY. There ain't no other key; I can
swear to that.
MAGEE. Good! *(Continues reading)* "This will
insure you against interruption, and give you the
solitude necessary for concentration. You are to
begin work at twelve o'clock Tuesday night, and
turn over to Mr. Elijah Quimby the completed manuscript of a ten-thousand-word story of Baldpate no
later than twelve o'clock Wednesday night." *(To*
QUIMBY) You understand?
QUIMBY. You're to turn it over to me?
MAGEE. Precisely.
QUIMBY. What do you think of that, Mother?
MRS. QUIMBY. I never heard of such a thing!
MAGEE. You know Bentley's handwriting; there's
his signature—see for yourself. *(Hands paper to*
MRS. QUIMBY. QUIMBYS *get up and read it together.* MAGEE *takes stage.)*
QUIMBY. It's his writin', ain't it, Mother?
MRS. QUIMBY. *(Doubtfully)* Looks like it, but—
(Looks at MAGEE *suspiciously.)*

20   SEVEN KEYS TO BALDPATE

QUIMBY. *(Aside)* But what?
MRS. QUIMBY. *(Aside)* The whole thing don't sound right to me.
QUIMBY. *(Aside)* Me neither. We'd better watch this cuss.
MRS. QUIMBY. *(Aside)* I think so, too.

(QUIMBY *puts chair up* R. MRS. QUIMBY *goes toward table* L. *'Phone rings.* MRS. QUIMBY *runs to foot of stairs, screaming.* QUIMBY *hugs the desk, frightened.)*

MRS. QUIMBY. Good Lord!
QUIMBY. *(Over to* MAGEE, *up* C.) Did you hear that?
MAGEE. You mean the telephone?
MRS. QUIMBY. *(Runs to* MAGEE—QUIMBY *grabs* MAGEE *by the arms)* Spooks!
QUIMBY. Why, that thing's been out of commission all winter!

('Phone continues ringing. MAGEE *laughs.)*

MRS. QUIMBY. Let's get out of here, Lije.
MAGEE. *(Laughs)* Don't be alarmed, Mrs. Quimby; I think I can explain. Bentley has just about had the service renewed. He probably wants to find out if I've arrived. Excuse me just a moment. *(Goes to 'phone and stops buzzer.* QUIMBYS *stand* C., *watching.)* Hello, hello! . . . Yes. Yes, right on time. . . . Almost twenty minutes ago. . . . Half frozen, thank you. . . . Yes, he's here now, also Mrs. Quimby. . . . Oh, we understand each other perfectly well. . . . It's everything you said it was. . . . The lonesomest spot on earth is right. *(Laughs.)* You still feel that way about it, eh? Well, your opinion is going to cost you five thousand, old man. *(Laughs.)* All right, we'll see. . . .

You want to talk to him. . . . Just a second. *(To* QUIMBY*)* He wants to talk to you, Mr. Quimby.

QUIMBY. *(Goes over to 'phone)* Is it Mr. Bentley?

MAGEE. Yes, here you are. Sit right down. *(He hands* QUIMBY *receiver and goes* L.C., *taking notes.* MRS. QUIMBY *goes up* R. *and listens to 'phone conversation while watching* MAGEE.)

QUIMBY. *(In 'phone)* Hello! *(Smiles as he recognizes* BENTLEY'S *voice.)* Hello, Mr. Bentley. . . . Yes, sir; yes, sir. . . . I understand, sir. . . . At twelve o'clock? . . . Yes, sir. . . . Oh, I'll be right here waiting. . . . Fine, thank you, sir; we're both fine. . . . All right, sir. . . . Wait a minute. I'll ask him. *(To* MAGEE, *who is on first landing of stairs.)* He wants to know if there's anything more you want to say?

MAGEE. *(On stairs, taking notes)* No; just give him my regards, and tell him I'm spending his money already.

QUIMBY. *(In 'phone)* He says there's nothing else, sir. . . . Yes, sir, I understand. . . . Goodbye, sir. *(Hangs up receiver and crosses to* MAGEE.*)* He wants me to be here at twelve o'clock tomorrow night to talk to him on the telephone again.

MAGEE. *(Laughs as he goes to 'phone and severs connection)* And it's very sad news you'll impart to him, Mr. Quimby. I'm going to win this wager! *(*R., *below 'phone.)* You know this whole thing wouldn't make a bad story in itself. *(Crossing to* L.*)* I'm thinking seriously of using it for the ground plot. *(Points to door* L.*)* Oh, this leads to where? *(Goes to door of dining-room* L. *and opens it.)*

MRS. QUIMBY. *(Going over toward door)* That's the dining-room—leads through to the kitchen. That door to the left goes to the cellar. *(Goes back to table* L. QUIMBY *looks at his watch.)*

Magee. Ah, ha, I see! *(Goes toward* Quimby, r.c.*)* Have you the exact time, Mr. Quimby?
Quimby. Mine says half-past eleven.
Magee. Thirty minutes to get my bearings and frame up a character or two for a start. *(Crosses* c. *to* r.c.*)*
Mrs. Quimby. *(Picks up suitcase and machine case from table* l.*)* Will I put these in your room?
Magee. No, no; you needn't bother.
Mrs. Quimby. Oh, it's no bother at all. *(Starts for the stairs.)* I'm only too glad to do anything for any friend of Mr. Bentley. *(Climbs stairs with cases and exits into room* r.*)*
Magee. *(Up to* Quimby, l.c.*)* Now you're quite sure I won't be disturbed while I am writing?
Quimby. *(*l.c.*)* Who's goin' to disturb you here? No one ever comes within a mile of this place till around the first of April, except myself, and I only come up about once a week this kind of weather.
Magee. You don't suppose any of Bentley's Asquewan friends, hearing of the wager, would take it upon themselves to interrupt the progress of my work?
Quimby. Nobody knows you're here except me and the Missus, and we ain't goin' to tell no one.
Magee. I have your word for that? *(Offers his hand to* Quimby.*)*
Quimby. *(Takes* Magee's *hand)* I never broke my word in my life. Guess that's why I'm a poor man. (Magee *crosses to* r.c.*)* The only other time I remember of anybody comin' here in the winter was the time of the reform wave at Reuton. The reformers got after a lot of crooked politicians, and they broke in here in the middle of the night and hid a lot of graft money in that safe over there. *(Points to safe.* Magee *goes up to safe, opens the door, then comes down to* Quimby, *after closing safe door.)*

MAGEE. You mean to tell me the reformers hid money in that safe?
QUIMBY. No, the politicians. Reformers never have any money.
MAGEE. *(Laughs as he goes* R.*)* Splendid!
QUIMBY. What are you laughing at?
MAGEE. *(Turning back to* QUIMBY*)* Nothing; it's all right. Go on, tell me about the hidden graft.
QUIMBY. (MRS. QUIMBY *starts downstairs, bringing lantern and placing it on table* L.*)* Oh, there's nothing much to tell. Some fellers up and gave 'em away, and the police come the next morning and found it here. Nobody claimed it, so of course they never got the gang. They threw a lot of fellers out of office, I believe. I didn't read much about it. But that's over four years ago. You needn't be afraid, you won't be disturbed here. *(Goes* L. *to table and gets his mittens and cap.* MRS. QUIMBY *is at table putting on mittens, etc.)*
MAGEE. *(Going slightly* R.*)* Grafting politicians—reformers—hidden money! Sounds like a good seller.
MRS. QUIMBY. *(Goes to* MAGEE *at* C.—QUIMBY *takes lantern and goes back of table)* Is there anything more we can do for you, Mr. Magee?
MAGEE. No, nothing I can think of, thank you. I'll be quite—— *(Crossing to* QUIMBY *at table*—MRS. QUIMBY *to* R.C.*)* Oh, yes, of course. You've forgotten something, Mr. Quimby.
QUIMBY. Forgot what?
MAGEE. The key.
QUIMBY. Oh, Lord! Yes, the key! Here it is. *(Hands* MAGEE *the key.)*
MAGEE. You're positively certain that this key is the only key to Baldpate in existence?
QUIMBY. Yes, sir; I'm sure.
MRS. QUIMBY. I can swear to it.
MAGEE. Good!

Mrs. Quimby. What are you going to do, lock yourself in?

Magee. Precisely.

Quimby. I don't mind staying here and keepin' watch for you if you want me to.

Magee. No, thanks; I much prefer to be alone.

Mrs. Quimby. I'd rather it would be you than me. Lord, I should think you'd be afraid of ghosts.

Quimby. *(Crosses to* Mrs. Quimby*)* Mother, I've told you twenty times there ain't no such a thing. (Magee *goes up* L.*)*

Mrs. Quimby. Well, they've been seen here, just the same.

Magee. *(Goes* L.C. *to* Quimbys*)* Ghosts!

Quimby. Oh, don't mind her, Mr. Magee. We think we know what the ghost is. There's an old feller up here in the mountain by the name of Peters —he's a hermit.

Magee. A hermit!

Quimby. Yes; he's one of them fellers that's been disappointed in love. His wife run off with a traveling man. He come here about ten years ago—lives in a little shack about a mile and a half north of here; calls it the Hermit's Cave. All the summer boarders buy picture postcards from him. We figger he's the feller that's been frightening the people down in the valley by wavin' a lantern from the mountainside with a white sheet wrapped around him.

Mrs. Quimby. But no one ever proved it was him.

Quimby. Well, who else could it be? There ain't no such a thing as ghosts, is there, Mr. Magee?

Magee. Well, I hope not. *(Muses. By-play between the* Quimbys.*)* Ghosts—hermits—not bad at all!

Quimby. Well, come along, Mother; I guess maybe Mr. Magee is anxious to get to work. I'll say good-night, sir. *(Offers hand to* Magee.*)*

MAGEE. *(Shakes* QUIMBY'S *hand)* Good night. And remember, twelve o'clock sharp for Mr. Bentley's 'phone call to-morrow night.

QUIMBY. I'll be here on the minute. *(Goes up* C.*)*

MRS. QUIMBY. *(Shaking hands with* MAGEE*)* And I'm comin' to see if you're still alive. Lord, I should think you'd be scared to death.

QUIMBY. *(Comes down* L. *of* MAGEE*)* Mother, he will be if you keep on like that. Well, good night, sir, and good luck. *(Goes up toward door, followed by* MRS. QUIMBY.*)*

MAGEE. *(Goes up to door and unlocks it)* Good night. I don't envy you your trip down the mountain on a night like this. *(Opens door. Wind effect.)*

MRS. QUIMBY. Good night, sir. *(Starts through door, followed by* QUIMBY, *carrying lantern.)*

MAGEE. Good night, Mrs. Quimby. Keep a sharp lookout for ghosts and hermits. *(Laughs.)*

MRS. QUIMBY. *(Outside)* Lord, don't remind me, please!

MAGEE. *(Slams door quickly, locks it, waves his hand to the* QUIMBYS, *then stands looking at key in his hand)* The only one, eh? Humph, we'll see! *(Puts key in his pocket, looks around room, thinks, then claps his hands as if decided on something; grabs his coat and hat from chair near fire, extinguishes lamps and bracket lights, takes a last look around room, and then exits upstairs into room* R. *on balcony.)*

(Black Drop down for ten seconds. End of Prologue. Drop up for Act I. The clock strikes twelve. The sound of a typewriter is heard clicking from the room occupied by MAGEE. *A short pause of absolute silence, then* BLAND *appears at door, peering into room.)*

BLAND. (*Opens door, enters, locks door, then comes down to* C. *and looks about, rubbing his hands and blowing on them to warm them. Sees safe, goes up to it, tries the door, opens it, and goes down* R. *As he starts for 'phone he sees fire burning, and stops dead.*) A log fire! Who the devil built that? (*Thinks, snaps fingers, goes to 'phone and puts in plugs.*) 2875 West. Hurry it along, sister. (MAGEE *enters from room and stands on balcony listening, leaving door of room open. In 'phone*) Hello, is that you, Andy? . . . . This is Bland. . . . Yes, Baldpate. . . . Yes, damn near frozen. . . . Oh, awful! It's like Napoleon's tomb. . . . I thought you said Mayor Cargan would meet me here? . . . No, no, I can't stay here all night; I'd go mad. . . . Listen, I'll hide the money here in the safe, and meet him at nine o'clock in the morning and turn it over to him then. . . . There isn't a chance in the world of anything happening. . . . The money's safer here than any spot on earth. . . . I'll lock the safe as soon as I put the package in. . . . Mayor Cargan knows the combination. . . . My advice is to let it lay here a week. It's the last place they'll look for it. Besides, how could they get in? My key to Baldpate is the only one in existence. (MAGEE, *on balcony, takes out his key and looks at it*.) They don't figure we'd take the chance after the other exposure. I tell you I know best. . . . I'll be back in town by one o'clock. . . . I've got the president's machine waiting at the foot of the mountain. . . . All right; good-bye. (*Hangs up receiver, goes* C., *takes package of money from his pocket, looks at it and around room, then goes to safe and deposits the money therein.* MAGEE *starts slowly and stealthily downstairs.* BLAND *closes door of safe, turns the handle, tries doors to see if they are locked securely, then comes down to fireplace and warms himself. As he turns his back to the fire, he comes face to face* with Magee, *who by this time is standing* R. Bland's *hand goes to his pocket for his gun as he comes slowly* C. *to* Magee.)

Magee. *(Cool and collected)* Good evening—or perhaps I should say, good morning.

Bland. *(Keeping his hand on gun as he advances toward* Magee*)* Who are you?

Magee. I was just about to put that question to you.

Bland. What are you doing here?

Magee. I rather think I'm the one entitled to an explanation.

Bland. Did you follow me up that mountain?

Magee. Oh, no; I was here an hour ahead of you.

Bland. How'd you get in here?

Magee. *(Points)* Through that door.

Bland. You lie! There's only one key to that door, and I have it right here in my pocket.

Magee. My dear sir, I was laboring under that same impression until a moment ago; but as your key fits the lock, and my key fits the lock, there are evidently two keys to Baldpate instead of one. *(He shows* Bland *his key.)* See?

Bland. You mean to tell me that's a key to Baldpate?

Magee. Yes. That's why I became so interested in your arrival here. I heard you telephone your friend just now and declare that your key was the only one in existence. *(Laughs.)* It sort of handed me a laugh.

Bland. You heard what I said over the telephone?

Magee. Every word.

Bland. *(Pulls pistol)* You don't think you're going to live to tell it, do you?

Magee. Have no fear on that score. I'm not a tattle-tale, nor do I intend to pry into affairs that do not concern me. But I should like your answering me one question. Where did you get your key to Baldpate?

BLAND. None of your damned business! I didn't come here to tell you the story of my life!

MAGEE. Well, you might at least relate that portion of it that has led you to trespassing on a gentleman seeking seclusion.

BLAND. Trespassing, eh? Who's trespassing, you or I?

MAGEE. My right here is indisputable.

BLAND. Who gave you that key?

MAGEE. None of your damned business! If I remember rightly, that's the answer you gave me.

BLAND. *(Goes slightly nearer* MAGEE*)* You've got a pretty good nerve to talk like that with a gun in front of your face.

MAGEE. Oh, that doesn't disturb me in the least. While I have never experienced this sort of thing in real life before, I've written so much of this melodramatic stuff and collected such splendid royalties from it all, that it rather amuses me to discover that the so-called literary trash is the real thing, after all. You may not believe it, but, really, old chap, I've written you over and over again! *(Laughs heartily and slaps* BLAND *on the shoulder. The latter backs away after second slap.* MAGEE *sits at table, still laughing heartily.)*

BLAND. *(Up close to* MAGEE*)* Say, I killed a man once for laughing at me.

MAGEE. That's my line—I used it in "The Lost Limousine." Four hundred thousand copies. I'll bet you've read it.

BLAND. *(Pointing gun)* If you don't tell me who you are and what you're doing here, I'll kill you as dead as a door-nail. Come on, I mean business— who are you?

MAGEE. Well, a name doesn't mean so much, so you may call me Mr. Smith.
BLAND. What are you?
MAGEE. A writer of popular novels.
BLAND. What are you doing here?
MAGEE. Trying to win a bet by completing a story of Baldpate in twenty-four hours. *(Gets up.)* A few more interruptions of this sort, however, and it's plain to be seen I'll pay the winner. *(Up close to* BLAND.) You can do me a big favor, old man, by leaving me this place to myself for the night. I give you my word of honor that whatever I've seen or heard shall remain absolutely sacred.
BLAND. *(Sneeringly)* You must think I'm an awful fool to swallow that kind of talk!
MAGEE. Very well, if you don't believe I'm who I say I am, and you doubt that I'm here for the reason I gave, go upstairs into that room with the open door—*(Points to room* R. *on balcony.* BLAND *looks up and backs away)*—and you'll find a typewriting machine, several pages of manuscript scattered about the floor, and a letter on the dresser from the owner of this inn to the caretaker, proving conclusively that all I've told you is the truth and nothing but the truth, and there you are.
BLAND. *(Up close to* MAGEE*)* And you're not in with the police?
MAGEE. No. I wish I were, if the graft is as good as they say it is.
BLAND. You say you have a letter from the owner of the inn?
MAGEE. Yes. Wait a minute, and I'll get it for you. *(Starts upstairs, but is stopped by* BLAND *as he is about halfway up.)*
BLAND. *(Shouts)* Come back!
MAGEE. *(Comes down and goes to* L.C.*)* What's the matter?
BLAND. *(Going* L.C. *to* MAGEE*)* I've been double-

crossed before, young fellow. I'll find it if it's there.

MAGEE. Oh, very well. If you prefer to get it yourself, why, go right along. *(He turns from* BLAND. *As he does so,* BLAND *fans him for a gun.* MAGEE *turns, surprised; then, as he understands, he laughs.)* You needn't be alarmed; I never carried a gun in my life.

BLAND. But you keep one in your room, eh?

MAGEE. If you think so, search the room.

BLAND. That's just what I'm going to do. I guess I'll keep you in sight, though. Go on; I'll let you show me the way.

MAGEE. All right. *(Starts toward stairs.)* If that's the way you feel about it, why, certainly. *(Goes upstairs leisurely, followed by* BLAND, *who keeps him covered.* MAGEE *starts to exit into room.* BLAND *stops him.)*

BLAND. (c. *of balcony)* Wait a minute; I'll peek around that room alone first. You don't look good to me; you're too damned willing. *(Goes to door of room* R. MAGEE *steps out to* R. *of door.)* You wait out here. I'll call you when I've satisfied myself you're not trying to spring something.

MAGEE. Very well. If you don't trust me, go ahead.

(BLAND *exits into room, keeping his eyes fixed on* MAGEE. *The latter stands thinking for a moment, then turns and slams door quickly, locks it, and runs downstairs to 'phone. When he is halfway down* BLAND *starts hammering on door.)*

BLAND. *(Yelling and hammering on door)* Open this door! *(Hammers.)* Damn you, I'll get you for this!

MAGEE. *(At 'phone)* Hello, I want to talk to the

Asquewan police headquarters. . . . That's what I said, police headquarters.

(BLAND *pounds on door. As* MAGEE *sits waiting for connection,* MARY NORTON *appears at door. She unlocks it and enters, closing door. The cold blast of wind attracts* MAGEE, *who jumps up and yells:)*

MAGEE. Who's there? What do you want?
MARY. Don't shoot; it's all right. I'm harmless.
MAGEE. How did you open that door?
MARY. *(Slightly down toward* MAGEE) Unlocked it with a key, of course.
MAGEE. *(Half aside)* My God!
MARY. *(Comes toward* MAGEE) If you will allow me to bring my chaperon inside, I will explain in a moment who I am and why we're here.
MAGEE. Your chaperon!
MARY. *(Going up to door)* Yes; another perfectly harmless female who has been kind enough to accompany me on this wild adventure. *(Turns to* MAGEE) I have your permission?
MAGEE. *(Looks up at room* R., *then back at* MARY, *puzzled)* Say, what the deuce is this all about?
MARY. You'll soon know. *(Opens door and calls)* All right, Mrs. Rhodes.

(MRS. RHODES *screams off stage, then enters and runs past* MARY *to above table* L., *terribly frightened.)*

MAGEE. What's the matter? What's happened?
MRS. RHODES. *(Shouting to* MARY) Lock the door! Lock the door!

(MARY *hurriedly locks door.)*

Magee. *(Crosses to* Mrs. Rhodes, *speaking hurriedly)* Tell me, please, what is it?

Mary. *(Runs down* L. *to* Mrs. Rhodes) What frightened you, Mrs. Rhodes?

Mrs. Rhodes. *(Almost hysterical)* A man!

Magee. A man?

Mary. What man?

Mrs. Rhodes. I don't know. He appeared at the window above, flourishing a revolver, and then he jumped to the ground and started running down the mountain-side.

Magee. Are you sure?

Mrs. Rhodes. Of course I'm sure.

Magee. Just a moment. *(Turns and darts upstairs, taking key from his pocket as he goes.)*

Mary. *(Going* R.C. *with* Mrs. Rhodes) Is there anything wrong?

Magee. I'm beginning to think I am. *(Opens door* R. *on balcony and exits.)*

Mrs. Rhodes. *(Still hysterical)* Why did you ever come here?

Mary. *(Coolly)* It's all right. Don't get excited.

Magee. *(Enters from room* R. *and comes to* C. *of balcony)* The bird has flown, but he forgot this when he took the jump. *(Points gun at women.* Mrs. Rhodes *runs* R., *screaming;* Mary *screams and runs* L.) Don't be alarmed; I'm not going to shoot—at least, not yet. *(Is on landing of stairs as he speaks next lines.)* Now might I ask why I'm so honored by this midnight visit? *(Snaps on bracket lights and comes down* C.)

Mary. *(Goes* L.C. *to* Magee) I can explain in a very few words.

Magee. That will suit me immensely. My time is valuable. I'm losing thousands of dollars, perhaps, through even this waste of time. *(Looks at*

SEVEN KEYS TO BALDPATE 33

Mary *intently.)* Be as brief as possible, please. I—— *(Stares at her.)*
MARY. Why do you stare at me so?
MAGEE. Do you believe in love at first sight?

(MRS. RHODES *takes a step toward them, surprised.)*

MARY. What do you mean?
MAGEE. You know, I've written about it a great many times, but I never believed in it before. It's really remarkable! *(Looks from* MARY *to* MRS. RHODES, *puzzled; then laughs in an embarrassed manner.)* Oh, pardon me, you were about to explain your visit here.
MARY. Well, to begin with, I—— *('Phone rings. All turn and look at it.)*
MAGEE. *(Goes to 'phone, stops buzzer, then backs upstage* C. MRS. RHODES *is* R.C. *To* MARY) Will you be kind enough to answer that 'phone? I don't care to turn my back on anything but a bolted door to-night. *(As* MARY *looks surprised.)* If you please.
MARY. Certainly. *(Goes to 'phone.* MRS. RHODES *goes* R.C., *above* MARY.) Hello! . . . What's that? . . . Hold the wire, please, I'll see. *(Turns to* MAGEE.) Did you wish to talk to police headquarters?
MRS. RHODES. *(Goes to* MAGEE C., *frightened)* Police headquarters!
MAGEE. *(Crossing* MRS. RHODES, *who goes over to* R. *of table* L.) Yes. *(Starts, then stops and looks up at room* R. *on balcony.)* But, no; just say they must have made a mistake. *(Backs upstage* C.)
MARY. *(In 'phone)* Hello! . . . No, no such call put in from here. Must be some mistake. That's all right. *(Stands up receiver and goes* L. MAGEE *goes to 'phone, severs connection, then comes down* C. MARY *up to him.)* Then you did call police headquarters?

MAGEE. I did.
MRS. RHODES. *(Goes to* C.*)* Why did you call police headquarters?
MARY. Yes, why did you call police headquarters?
MAGEE. *(Looks at both, puzzled, then laughs)* You know, these are the most remarkable lot of happenings. No sooner do I get rid of one best seller, than along comes another dyed-in-the-wool "to-be-continued-in-our-next." *(To* MARY*)* You know there's no particular reason for my saying this, but I really believe I'd do anything in the world for you.
MARY. I don't understand.
MAGEE. But you promised to explain your presence here.
MARY. Which I fully intend to do; but first of all I should like to ask you one question.
MAGEE. Proceed.
MARY. How did you get in here without this key? *(Shows him her key.)*
MAGEE. *(Laughs)* Oh, no, no! *(Laughs.)* You know, I'm beginning to think this whole thing is a frame-up.
MARY. What do you mean?
MAGEE. *(Points to her key)* You have the only key to Baldpate in existence, I suppose?
MARY. So I understood.
MAGEE. Well, if it's any news to you, ladies, believe me, there are more keys to Baldpate than you'll find in a Steinway piano.
MARY. Then he lied!
MAGEE. Who lied?
MRS. RHODES. *(Quickly)* Remember your promise, Mary! *(Crosses to chair in front of fire and sits.)*
MAGEE. *(Follows* MRS. RHODES *with his eyes, making complete turn.)* Well?
MARY. I can't tell you his name.

SEVEN KEYS TO BALDPATE 35

MAGEE. Well, at least tell me your name.
MARY. My name is Mary Norton. I do special stories for the "Reuton Star."
MAGEE. *(Surprised)* In the newspaper game?
MARY. That's it. And this lady—— *(Pointing to* MRS. RHODES, *who is now removing her rubbers.)* —is Mrs. Rhodes, with whom I live in Reuton, and who is the only other person who knows I'm here to do this story.
MAGEE. What story?
MARY. The story of the five-thousand-dollar wager you have made with a certain gentleman that you would write a complete novel inside of twenty-four hours.
MAGEE. Who told you this?
MRS. RHODES. Remember your promise, Mary.
MAGEE. *(Crosses to* R.C. MARY *goes* L.C. MAGEE *looks at* MRS. RHODES *and then at* MARY*)* You've made many a promise, haven't you, Mary? I should certainly like to know who gave you this information.
MARY. *(Goes to* MAGEE R.C.*)* I can tell you only that when the wager was made at the Forty-fourth street club this afternoon, a certain someone dispatched the news to me at once. Believing that I had the only key to Baldpate, I hurried here to let you in, and lo and behold—— *(Takes stage* L., MAGEE *following her.)*—I find you already at work, and as snug and cozy as you would be in a New York apartment. *(Comes down* R. *of table,* MAGEE *following her.)* Now that you know my story, I am going to throw myself on your mercy and ask you to allow me to stay here and get the beat. I promise you we shall not disturb you in the least. Have you any obections?
MAGEE. And you won't tell me who gave you the story?
MARY. I can't.

MAGEE. Nor where you got the key?
MRS. RHODES. Remember your promise, Mary.
MAGEE. *(Turns and looks at* MRS. RHODES *and then at* MARY*)* You know, I wish you hadn': brought her with you.
MRS. RHODES. What! *(Gets up and starts L toward* MAGEE.*)*
MAGEE. *(Goes toward her as she starts up)* No offense, Mrs. Rhodes. Of course I understand tha· Mary is a very promising young woman, but why continually remind her of the fact. *(Laughs apologetically.)* That's just my little joke. Excuse me *(Goes to* MARY C. MRS. RHODES *goes to window looking out.)* Let me get this clear. Your idea is to stop here and write the story of my twenty-fou₁ hour task?
MARY. With your permission.
MAGEE. Well, I'll tell you. Had you put such a proposition up to me—(MRS. RHODES *comes down stage to* R.C.*)*—half an hour ago, I should have said emphatically, no; but since my little experience with the gun-flourishing, window-jumping gentleman, I'm inclined to entertain the idea of a companion or two
MRS. RHODES. *(R. of* MAGEE*)* Who was the man with the gun?
MARY. Why did he jump from the window?
MAGEE. You might as well ask me why he placed a package of money in that safe. (MARY *and* MRS RHODES *go up toward safe.)* Or why he telephoned the fact to someone else, who was to pass the word along to Mayor Cargan.
MRS. RHODES. *(Turns to* MAGEE, *amazed)* Mayo₁ Cargan!
MAGEE. What seems to be the trouble?
MARY. *(To* MAGEE, C.*)* Mrs. Rhodes is a widow; Mayor Cargan a widower. Perhaps you will understand why the name startled her when]

SEVEN KEYS TO BALDPATE

tell you that Mrs. Rhodes is to become Mrs. Cargan next Sunday morning.

MAGEE. Oh, indeed! (MARY *goes up* C., *then down again during next speech.* MAGEE *crosses to* MRS. RHODES.) Well, congratulations, Mrs. Rhodes. And again I say I did not mean to offend. I am not accusing Mayor Cargan of any transaction, dishonest or otherwise. I was merely trying to point out to you ladies that it has been a night of wild occurrences up to now. However, if you care to take the risk, stay here. It won't disturb me in the least, and may possibly benefit this young lady in her business. (*Goes toward* MARY. *Looks at his watch and whistles.*) I've lost half an hour already, and as every minute means money to me right now, I'll have to work fast to make up for the time I've lost. (*To* MRS. RHODES—MARY *comes down* L.C.) Again I apologize for any mistake I may have made, Mrs. Rhodes.

MRS. RHODES. I assure you a more honest man than Jim Cargan never lived.

MAGEE. I sincerely trust you're right, especially for your own sake. (MRS. RHODES *sits in front of fire.* MAGEE *goes to* MARY *and takes her hand.*) I hope the story proves a whale. I wish——

MARY. What do you wish?

MAGEE. Oh, nothing—I was just thinking of Sunday morning. Good-night.

MARY. Good-night.

MAGEE. (*As he goes up the stairs*) I'd gladly offer you ladies my room, but it's the only one cleaned and heated, and I must have some comfort for this kind of work. (*On balcony* R.) Good-night, ladies.

MARY *and* MRS. RHODES. Good-night.

MAGEE. (*Leaning over balcony*) Mary—that's the sweetest name in the world.

MARY. (*Looking up at him*) Thank you.

MAGEE. Good-night.

MARY. Good-night.
MAGEE. *(A long look at* MARY *and then at* MRS. RHODES) I still wish you hadn't brought her with you. Good-night.
MARY. Good-night.

(MAGEE *exits into room* R. *on balcony, closing door.)*

MRS. RHODES. *(Over to* MARY, R.C.) You don't believe Jim Cargan guilty of any treachery? Tell me you don't, Mary.
MARY. I don't know, Mrs. Rhodes. I told you of the Suburban bribe story we got last night, but I certainly hope the name of Cargan is kept clean, for both your sakes.
MRS. RHODES. I can't believe he's wrong! I won't believe it! *(Crosses to* L.C.*)*
MARY. *(Following* MRS. RHODES) But if he is wrong, it's best you should know it now. The fates may have brought us here to-night to protect you; who knows?
MRS. RHODES. *(Going toward safe)* Money hidden in that safe, he said.
MARY. Yes, and that dovetails with the Suburban bribe story. *(Both come down stage a trifle.)* I came down here to do a special. I may get two sweeps with the one broom. Wouldn't that be wonderful? I'd be made!
MRS. RHODES. *(Turns upstage, looks toward door, and sees* PETERS) Great Heavens, Mary, look!
MARY. What is it? *(Looks up at door, sees* PETERS, *screams, and runs* L. *behind banister.* MRS. RHODES *screams and runs* R. *and hides behind chair.* MAGEE *enters on balcony after second scream.)*
MAGEE. *(Looking down at women)* What's wrong down there?
MRS. RHODES. A ghost!
MAGEE. What!

SEVEN KEYS TO BALDPATE

MARY. A ghost! A ghost!
MAGEE. *(Laughing)* I'll bet you four dollars that's the fellow whose wife ran away with a traveling man! *(Starts to come downstairs.)*
MARY and MRS. RHODES. *(They wave MAGEE back)* Ssh!

(MAGEE *snaps out lights.* PETERS *unlocks the door, enters, locks door, then throws the sheet over his arm and comes down stage, looking from* MARY *to* MRS. RHODES, *who both come forward a trifle.* MAGEE *comes to* L. *of* PETERS *at* C.)

MAGEE. I beg your pardon; but have you any idea just how many keys there are to this flat?
PETERS. *(Ignores question)* What are these women doing here?
MAGEE. How's that?
PETERS. I don't like women.

(MRS. RHODES *and* MARY *scream and run to foot of stairs.)*

MAGEE. It's all right, ladies; he's not a regular ghost. I know all about him. He's in the picture-postcard business.
PETERS. *(Gruffly)* What!
MAGEE. *(To* PETERS) Just a minute, Bosco. *(To ladies)* If you ladies will kindly step upstairs into my room, I'll either kill it or cure it. *(Ladies go up and stand on balcony.)*
PETERS. *(Gruffly)* What?
MAGEE. *(To* PETERS) See here, that's the second time you've barked at me. Now don't do it again, do you hear? *(To ladies)* Go right in, ladies. *(They exit into room* R., *closing door.* MAGEE *down to* PETERS.) So you're the ghost of Baldpate, are you?

PETERS. How'd you people get in here?

MAGEE. *(Laughs)* You're not going to pull that "only key in existence" speech on me, are you?

PETERS. What?

MAGEE. You know there are other keys besides yours.

PETERS. They're all imitations. Mine's the real key. The old man gave it to me the day before he died.

MAGEE. What old man?

PETERS. The father of that young scamp who wastes his time around those New York clubs. You know who I mean.

MAGEE. Then you're not particularly fond of the present owner of Baldpate?

PETERS. I hate him and all his men friends.

MAGEE. You don't like women either, you say.

PETERS. I despise them!

MAGEE. How do little girls and boys strike you?

PETERS. Bah!

MAGEE. *(Laughs)* I can understand your wife now—anything in preference to you, even a traveling man!

PETERS. Don't mention my wife's name, or I'll— *(Raises lantern to strike* MAGEE.*)*

MAGEE. *(Pulls lantern out of* PETERS' *hand)* Now, see here, old man, if you make any more bluffs at me I'll take that white sheet away from you and put you right out of the ghost business. Haven't you any better sense than to go about frightening little children this way? Why don't you stick to your own line of work? You're a hermit by trade, if I'm rightly informed.

PETERS. Yes, I'm a hermit, and proud of it.

MAGEE. Then why don't you cut out this ghost stuff and be a regular hermit?

PETERS. I play the ghost because I love to see the cowards run.

SEVEN KEYS TO BALDPATE

MAGEE. Oh, they're all cowards—is that it?
PETERS. Cowards, yes! *(Laughs gruffly.)*
MAGEE. And you're a brave man, I suppose?
PETERS. A cave man is always a brave man.

(Pistol shots heard outside, then a woman's scream. PETERS *laughs and dances up to door and peers through.)*

PETERS. Ha, ha! They're shooting again! They're shooting again!

*(*MARY *and* MRS. RHODES *have come out on balcony at shots.)*

MAGEE. *(Up to door and peers through)* What's that?
MARY. What's happened?
MRS. RHODES. Is someone hurt? *(Both lean over balcony, looking down.)*
MAGEE. Did you hear a woman scream?
MARY. *(Frightened)* Distinctly.
MRS. RHODES. *(Frightened)* And a pistol shot!
PETERS. *(Dramatically, as he goes toward door* L. *slowly)* A woman in white—a woman in white! They shot at her as they shoot at me when I play the ghost. *(Laughs.)* They thought it was the ghost. *(Almost whispers.)* Thought it was the ghost. *(Laughs viciously and exits door* L.*)*

*(*MYRA THORNHILL *appears at door* C. *and is seen unlocking it.)*

MAGEE. *(Runs to foot of stairs and calls up to women)* My God, another key!
MARY *and* MRS. RHODES. What?
MAGEE. Ssh! It's a woman! *(He waves them back.)* Ssh!

(MARY and MRS. RHODES *go back into room* R. MA-
GEE *crouches behind banister, unseen by* MYRA
until he speaks. MYRA *enters, locks doors, then
tiptoes cautiously to dead* C. *She takes a sweep-
ing glance around, then goes to fire and warms
herself; comes to* C. *again, and on making sure
that no one is in the room, she goes to safe and
starts working combination, first picking up lantern from desk and holding it in her left hand,
while working combination with her right.)*

MAGEE. *(Snapping on bracket lights)* I thought
I'd give you a little more light so you could work
faster. (MYRA *puts lantern on desk and throws up
her hands.)* You needn't throw up your hands; I'll
take a chance on that quick stuff. Come on out here,
please. *(Laughs as* MYRA *comes around desk* R. *to*
C. *slowly.)* I didn't think they did that sort of thing
outside of melodrama and popular novels, but I see
I was wrong, or I should say right, when I wrote it.
(MYRA *continues to advance to him slowly.)* Really,
you're the most attractive burglar I've ever seen.
That is, if you are a burglar. Are you?

MYRA. *(Coolly)* Are you one of the Cargan
crowd, or do you represent the Reuton Suburban
people?

(MARY *and* MRS. RHODES *enter on balcony and
listen.)*

MAGEE. No, I'm just an ordinary man trying to
win a bet; but up to now the chances have been dead
against me. Perhaps you'd like to tell me who you
are.

MYRA. I will, if you'll answer me one question.

MAGEE. *(Laughs)* Of course, of course. I'll answer that one before you ask it. A friend of mine gave it to me. Of course you thought you had the only one in existence, but he lied to you. I have a cute little key of my own. Oh, there are keys and keys, but I love my little key best of all. *(Shows her his key, kissing it.)* See?

MYRA. I can't understand it at all.

MAGEE. You haven't anything on me. And just about two more keys, and I'll pack up my paraphernalia, go back to New York, and never make another bet as long as I live!

MYRA. *(Up close to him)* Will you please tell me your name?

MAGEE. Well, a name doesn't mean so much, so you may call me Mr. Jones. And yours?

MYRA. My name is—— *(Hesitates.* MARY *and* MRS. RHODES *lean over balcony, listening.)* Listen! *(Brings* MAGEE *downstage.)* My husband is the president of the Asquewan-Reuton Suburban Railway Company. He has agreed to pay a vast amount of money for a certain city franchise; a franchise that the political crowd at Reuton has no power to grant. They are going to cheat him out of this money and use it for campaign funds to fight the opposition party at the next election. If he sues for his money back, they are going to expose him for entering into an agreement he knows to be nothing short of bribery. The present mayor is at the bottom of it all. *(*MARY *and* MRS. RHODES *start at mention of mayor's name.)* I ran to my husband to-night and begged him not to enter into this deal. I warned him that he was being cheated. He wouldn't believe me, but I know it's true. He's being cheated, and will be charged with bribery besides. That's why I risked the mountain on a night like this. I must have been followed, for I was shot at as I reached the top of Baldpate. Oh, I don't know who you are, but you're a man and you can help me. *(Puts her hands on his shoulders, pleadingly.)* You will help me, won't you?

MAGEE. *(Interested)* Yes. What do you want me to do?

MYRA. *(Looks at MAGEE for a moment without speaking, then goes up to safe and back to MAGEE)* In that safe there is a package containing two hundred thousand dollars.

MAGEE. *(Goes up toward safe)* Two hundred thousand dollars!

(MARY *and* MRS. RHODES *start downstairs very slowly.)*

MYRA. *(Following MAGEE up R.)* That's the amount. It must be there. A man named Bland was to bring it here and deposit it at midnight. Cargan was to follow later, and was to find it here.

MAGEE. *(Coming down stage)* Cargan coming here!

MYRA. So they've planned it. I must have that money out of there before he arrives. You'll help me, won't you? Don't you understand? My husband is being cheated, tricked, robbed, probably ruined.

MAGEE. But I don't know the combination.

MYRA. *(Wringing her hands)* Oh, there must be something we can do! Please, please—— *(She kneels at his feet and puts up her hands imploringly.)* For the sake of my children, help me, please! (MAGEE *sees women on stairs, and warns* MYRA *with a look as he helps her to her feet. She turns and faces* MARY *and* MRS. RHODES, *then turns abruptly to* MAGEE.) Who are these women? What are they doing here? *(She has changed from hysteria to dignified coldness.)*

MAGEE. Oh, of course, pardon me! *(Goes to*

women at foot of stairs. MYRA *crosses to* R.) May I introduce Miss——
MYRA. *(Cuts him off sharply)* Please don't! *(Turns to women.)* Will you pardon me for a moment, ladies?
MARY *and* MRS. RHODES. Certainly. *(They step off stairs and remain* L., *keeping their eyes fixed on* MYRA *and* MAGEE. MAGEE *goes* R. *to* MYRA.)
MYRA. *(Aside to* MAGEE) For God's sake, don't tell them who I am. My husband will kill me if he ever learns that I've been here on such an errand.
MAGEE. *(Aside)* I understand; you may trust me. I sympathize with you very deeply, Madam, and I promise you that no one shall take that money away from here to-night unless it be yourself. And I'll get it out of that safe if I have to blow the thing to smithereens!
MYRA. You give me your word as a gentleman?
MAGEE. *(Offers his hand)* My word as a gentleman.
MYRA. *(Takes his hand)* Thank you.
MAGEE. *(Pulls down his vest and goes up to* MARY *and* MRS. RHODES) Ladies, I wish to present a girl schoolmate of mine, Miss Brown, who has become interested enough in my career to find her way to Baldpate to witness my endeavor to break all records as a speedy story-writer.
MARY *and* MRS. RHODES. Miss Brown. *(Both bow.* MYRA *returns the bow.)*
MAGEE. *(Takes out his watch and looks at it)* Up to now I'm almost an hour behind myself. However, I expect to catch up with myself before the night is over. That is, of course, provided there aren't over three hundred more keys to the old front door.
MARY. *(Goes up to* MAGEE C.) Now, might I have a word with you alone?

MAGEE. I'd be delighted. I'd like to be alone with you forever.

MARY. (*To* MYRA) Will you pardon me for a moment?

MYRA. Certainly.

MAGEE. Go right upstairs, Miss Brown, and make yourself quite at home. (*Starts toward stairs with* MYRA.) Oh, Mrs. Rhodes, will you be good enough to show her to the room? (MARY *crosses* C. *to* R.) I'm sure she needs a little drop of something after that bitter cold trip up the mountain. You'll find a flask on the table.

MRS. RHODES. (*Starts up the stairs*) Come right along, Miss. I know where it is; I've already tried it. (*Exits room* R.)

MYRA. (*Following* MRS. RHODES *upstairs*) Well, really, I don't know what to say to all this kindness. I—— (*Stops* C. *on balcony, looks down and warns* MAGEE *to silence with finger on her lips. He reassures her, then goes* C.)

MRS. RHODES. (*Appearing at door*) Right in here, Miss.

MYRA. Thanks, awfully. (*Exits into room, followed by* MRS. RHODES, *who closes door.*)

MARY. (*Goes quickly to* MAGEE *at* C.) Who did that woman claim to be?

MAGEE. That's a secret I've promised never to reveal.

MARY. But I overheard everything she said.

MAGEE. Then you know.

MARY. I know she lied.

MAGEE. She lied!

MARY. She claimed to be the wife of Thomas Hayden, president of the Suburban Railway. She lied, I tell you. Why, I've known Mrs. Hayden all my life; was brought up and went to school with her daughters. Mrs. Hayden is a woman in her fifties. You can see for yourself that she is nothing more

than a slip of a girl. There's a mystery here of some kind—someone's playing a desperate game. *(Goes upstage excitedly, looking up at door R.)*
MAGEE. Yes, and it's costing me five thousand dollars. I'll never get my work done to-night, I can see that right now. *(Looks at watch.* MARY *comes down* C.*)* But what do I care? I've met you!
MARY. You're going to give this money over to that woman?

*(*PETERS *enters from L. and hides behind banisters.)*

MAGEE. Not if she lied.
MARY. Well, you believe me, don t you?
MAGEE. *(Takes her hand)* Believe you! Let me tell you something, little girl. I've written a lot of those Romeo speeches in my novels, though I never really felt this way before, but here goes: The moment you walked through that door to-night and I laid eyes on you, I made up my mind that you were the one woman in the world for me. Why, there's nothing I wouldn't do for you. Try me.
MARY. Very well, I shall. Get me that package of money out of that safe before Cargan comes to steal it. Help me to reach Reuton without being molested, and I'll annihilate the graft machine with to-morrow's edition of the "Star." With that money to turn over to the proper authorities as proof of the deal, I'll wipe out the street car trust and the Cargan crowd with one swing of the pen. And just think, I'll save Mrs. Rhodes from an alliance with a thief! I know Cargan's crooked, always has been; but I must prove it before she'll break off the engagement. Great Scott! what a story I'll write! Think what it will mean to me and to the city of Reuton itself! *(Puts her hands on his shoulders pleadingly.)* You will do this for me, won't you? Please, please!
MAGEE. Yes. What do you want me to do?

MARY. Come, we must hurry! Can't you think of some way to open that safe? *(Goes up toward safe,* MAGEE *following. He comes down* C.*)*

MAGEE. What are we going to do? We don't know the combination, and I haven't any dynamite. But we must have that $200,000.

(PETERS *moves chair just enough to betray his presence.)*

MARY. *(Comes down to* MAGEE, *frightened, placing her hand on his arm)* What was that?

MAGEE. Oh, that was nothing. It was just the wind creeping through the cracks, I fancy. *(Aside)* Go upstairs; there's someone hiding in this room. *(Aloud)* Good-night, Miss Norton.

MARY. Good-night. *(She hurries upstairs and exits into room* R.*)*

(MAGEE *looks around room for a moment, reaches over banisters and snaps out lights; starts whistling, and then goes upstairs to* L. *room on balcony, opens door, slams it loudly, and then comes out and sits behind banisters, watching* PETERS. PETERS *makes sure no one is in sight, then goes quickly over to safe and starts working combination quietly, but hurriedly,* MAGEE *watching him from stairs.* CARGAN *and* MAX *appear outside, peering through into room. As the safe door flies open, they enter quickly,* CARGAN *opening the door.* MAX *enters and goes quickly up* C. *and covers* PETERS *with gun.* CARGAN *closes door and goes quickly to* PETERS.*)*

MAX. Get away from that safe! (PETERS *jumps away.)* Put up your hands! (PETERS' *hands go up.)*

CARGAN. *(Recognizes him as he goes toward safe)*

"SEVEN KEYS TO BALDPATE" *See Page 44, Act I*

MYRA: "Who are these women? What are they doing here?"
Left to Right: Wm. Hallowell Magee, Myra Thornhill, Mary Norton, Mrs. Rhodes

Oh, it's you, is it? *(To* MAX) The ghost came near walking that time for fair! *(To* PETERS) Come out of there! (PETERS *comes in front of desk.)* How did you know the combination of that safe? *(No reply from* PETERS.) Who told you there was money in there? *(No reply from* PETERS.) Get out of here, you vagabond! *(Throws* PETERS *toward* L.*)* What do you mean by breaking into a man's safe in the middle of the night? Throw him in the cellar, Max.

MAX. Come on, hurry up! Get out! *(Throws* PETERS L.*)*

PETERS. *(At door* L.*)* Damn you, Cargan, I hate you!

CARGAN. Get out! *(Goes up and locks door.)*

MAX. Go on, get out!

(PETERS *exits* L. *door.* MAX *follows him off and returns almost immediately.)*

CARGAN. *(Goes to safe and gets package of money.* MAX *enters.)* By gad, we weren't any too soon! *(Goes to table* L.*)* Another moment, and he'd have had it sure. It would be good-bye to the hermit if he ever got hold of a roll like this! *(Flips bills in his hands.)* Two hundred one thousand dollar bills.

MAX. Is it all there?

CARGAN. I don't know; I'll see. (MAGEE *comes downstairs and goes behind desk while* MAX *and* CARGAN *are counting money.)* You seem surprised that I found the money here.

MAX. What do you mean—surprised?

CARGAN. *(Rises, puts money in his pocket, then comes in front of table.* MAX *comes forward and stands* L. *of* CARGAN, *below table.)* I'm going to tell you something, Max. I didn't trust you all day, and I didn't trust you to-night.

MAX. What do you mean—you didn't trust me?
CARGAN. I'll be truthful with you. I thought you were going to double cross me. I thought you were going to beat me to the bankroll through this woman Thornhill.
MAX. Myra Thornhill?
CARGAN. Yes, Myra Thornhill. Oh, don't play dead; you knew she was around. You've had secret meetings with her during the last forty-eight hours. I know every move you've made—I've had you watched. You've worked with her before. *(As* MAX *makes a motion of protest.)* You've told me so. I had my mind made up to kill you, Max, if this money had been gone, and that's just what I'm going to do if you ever double cross me, do you understand?
MAX. *(In a hangdog tone)* Yes, I understand.

(MAGEE, *who has been crouching between safe and desk, now stands up, takes aim, and fires at* L. *wall, then rushes over and turns on bracket lights. At the sound of the shot the women come out on balcony, frightened, and stand looking down at men.)*

CARGAN. *(As* MAGEE *shoots)* My God, I'm shot! *(Reels against table.* MAX *draws back* L.*)*
MAGEE. *(Comes down* R.C.*)* No, you're not. I just put a bullet into the wall, and I'll put one in you if you don't toss that package of money over here! Come on, hurry up! I mean business! (CARGAN *hesitates, then throws money to* MAGEE R.C. *The latter picks it up and puts it in his pocket.)* You see, being a writer of sensational novels, I'm well up in this melodramatic stuff.
MRS. RHODES. *(On balcony, watching* CARGAN*)* Jim Cargan!

SEVEN KEYS TO BALDPATE 51

CARGAN. *(He and* MAX *look up and see women on balcony)* What are you doing here? (MRS. RHODES *doesn't reply, but continues staring at him.)*

MYRA. *(Looking down at* MAX) Max, Max, are you hurt?

MAX. No; I'm all right.

CARGAN. *(Turning slowly to* MAX) Myra Thornhill, eh? So you were trying to cross me, you snake! *(Chokes* MAX. *Women scream.)*

MAGEE. I must insist upon orderly conduct, gentlemen. No roughhouse, please. *(To* MAX) Young man, be good enough to put that gun of yours on the table. (MAX *hesitates.)* Hurry now. (MAX *does as directed.)* Now kindly remove that gun from Mr. Cargan's pocket—I'm sure he has one—and put it on the table also. He might want to take a shot at you, and I'm giving you the necessary protection. Hurry, please.

(MAX *takes* CARGAN'S *gun and places it on table.)*

MAGEE. Now, Mrs. Rhodes, will you kindly ask the street car president's wife to step back into that room, then lock the door and remove the key? (MYRA *goes slowly to room* R. MRS. RHODES *follows her, locks the door, then comes to* C. *of balcony.)* Thank you. And now, Miss Norton, will you kindly step down here—(MARY *starts downstairs and hangs muff on chair* L.*)*—and take those two revolvers from the table and place them in the hotel safe, and then close the safe and turn the combination? (MARY *places guns in safe, turns combination, and remains up near desk.)* Thank you very much. *(To men)* Now, gentlemen, I must insist that you step upstairs to the room on the right of the balcony. And, Mrs. Rhodes, will you please step over there and lock the door when these gentlemen are on the other side? (MRS. RHODES *crosses bal-*

cony, goes to room L., *unlocks door, and stands aside for the men to pass in.)* I shan't keep you there long, gentlemen; I'll release you as soon as I've transacted some important business with this young lady. Lively, now, gentlemen! Lively! *(As men start upstairs slowly.)* That's it! Now to your right. Correct! Now straight ahead. (MAX *exits into room.* CARGAN *stops as he gets to door, and turns and looks appealingly at* MRS. RHODES, *who ignores his outstretched hands.)* Now right in. (CARGAN *exits into room* L.) Lock the door, Mrs. Rhodes, and bring the keys down to me. (MRS. RHODES *locks door and brings keys to* MAGEE *at* C.) That's the ticket! Thanks, very much. (MARY *comes to* C.) Well, how's my work? Some round-up, wasn't it? *(To* MRS. RHODES) I'm awfully sorry about this, for your sake, Mrs. Rhodes.
MARY. *(To* MAGEE, R. *of him)* It's best she should know. *(To* MRS. RHODES, *extending her hand.)* Isn't it, dear?
MRS. RHODES. *(Going* R.C., *after taking* MARY'S *hand)* I suppose so, dear, I suppose so.
MAGEE. Well, come on, little girl! You've got to work fast. Here's the graft money. *(Takes money from his pocket and gives it to* MARY.) Now what?
MARY. I've everything planned. I know just what I'm going to do. What's the time?
MAGEE. *(Looking at watch)* One-thirty. But you can't get a train out of Asquewan until five.

(MARY *crosses to* L., *gets muff, and places money in it.)*

MRS. RHODES. We can't sit around the station for three hours, dear. (MARY *returns* L.C. *to* MAGEE.)
MAGEE. Try to get a taxi, or whatever sort of conveyance they have in the darned town; but what-

ever you do, get out of Asquewan as soon as you can.

MARY. You leave it to me; I'll find a way. Are you going to stay here?

MAGEE. *(Looks up at room R. and L.)* I'll have to. I want to keep guard on this crowd of lady and gentleman bandits until I'm sure you're well on your way. I'll keep them here until you 'phone and tell me you're out of danger, even though it's all night to-night and all day to-morrow.

MARY. But your work?

MAGEE. Never mind the work; I can write a novel any old time. So far as the bet is concerned, I can lose that and still be repaid a million times over— I've met you. *(Takes her hand, then crosses to* MRS. RHODES. MARY *goes up* C.) Good-night, Mrs. Rhodes, and God bless you both!

MRS. RHODES. Good-night. *(Shakes hands with* MAGEE, *then starts for door and stands looking up at door* L. *on balcony.)*

MAGEE. *(To* MARY, *near door)* I wonder if we'll ever meet again?

MARY. I live in Reuton—good-night. *(Turns up near foot of stairs and looks up at door* L. MRS. RHODES *exits.)*

MAGEE. Good-night. (MARY *comes to door* MAGEE *is holding open. She pauses for a moment, looks at him intently, then down at floor, then exits quickly.* MAGEE *locks door, stands peering out at them for a moment, looks up at door* L., *then comes down stage and stands thinking.)* Crooked politicians—adventuress—safe robbed—love at first sight! *(Points to different rooms and at safe.)* And I wanted to get away from melodrama! *(Hears* HAYDEN *at door, and backs away to foot of stairs.)* And still they come!

(HAYDEN *enters, locks doors, puts key in his pocket,*

takes off gloves, rubs his hands and nose trying to warm them, then comes down to fireplace and stands with his back to the fire. As he turns he comes face to face with MAGEE, *who has come to* C. *He goes to* MAGEE *slowly.)*

HAYDEN. I beg pardon, but who are you?
MAGEE. *(C.)* I'm Mayor Cargan's butler.
HAYDEN. Mayor Cargan!
MAGEE. Yes, he's here. Do you wish to see him?
HAYDEN. *(Importantly)* Yes. Say to him that Mr. Hayden of the Reuton-Asquewan Suburban Road, is calling.
MAGEE. Oh, I see! Are you the president of that road, sir?
HAYDEN. *(Pompously)* I most certainly am, sir.
MAGEE. *(Looks at* HAYDEN, *and then up at room* R. *and laughs)* Your wife's here.
HAYDEN. What!
MAGEE. Yes; locked in that room up there. *(*MAGEE *points to room* R. *on balcony.* HAYDEN *turns and looks up. As he turns,* MAGEE *fans him for gun.* HAYDEN *turns to* MAGEE *quickly, sputtering.)* Pardon me, I just wanted to see if you had a gun on you. Just a minute; I'll tell the mayor the president has arrived. *(Starts upstairs, laughing.)*
HAYDEN. *(When* MAGEE *is on first landing)* Are you a crazy man, sir?
MAGEE. That's what the critics say, but I'm beginning to think they are all wrong. Sit down, Mr. Hayden. I'll tell the boys you're here. *(Unlocks door* L. *and steps aside.)*
HAYDEN. The boys!
MAGEE. Come on, boys; everything's all right; the president's here. *(As men come down,* HAYDEN *steps forward toward stairs.)* Watch your step. Easy, that's it; one at a time, please. Lead on, boys. I'll walk a little behind.

(CARGAN *and* MAX *come downstairs, followed by* MAGEE, *who covers them with gun. As men get to foot of stairs,* HAYDEN *backs away, thunderstruck.* MAX *goes to table* L. MAGEE *goes over* R. CARGAN *comes down to* HAYDEN C.)

CARGAN. *(Gruffly)* Hello, Hayden.
HAYDEN. What is the meaning of this, Cargan?
CARGAN. I don't know. Ask him. *(Nods toward* MAGEE.)
HAYDEN. *(To* CARGAN) Who is he?
CARGAN. I don't know, and I don't care a damn! I'm disgusted with the whole works. We're nailed, that's all I know. *(Sits* R. *of table* L. PETERS *enters from door* L. *On seeing crowd of men, he starts to back out, but is stopped by* MAGEE.)
MAGEE. No, you don't! Come back here. I'll keep my eye on you, too. You'd better sit down and join the boys, Hermy. (PETERS *sits* L. *of table.)*
HAYDEN. *(Up to* MAGEE, *who is* R.C.) I'd very much like to know the reason for such strange actions, young man?
MAGEE. Your wife will be down in a minute; she'll probably tell you all about it.
HAYDEN. Confound it, sir, my wife is home in bed!
MAGEE. That's what you think. *(Laughs.)* You're not the first fellow that's been fooled, you know. (HAYDEN *backs away from* MAGEE. MAGEE *throws key to* PETERS.) Here, Hermy; take that key and open the first door to the left on the balcony, and tell Mrs. Hayden that her husband wants to see her downstairs right away. *(As* PETERS *hesitates)* Hurry along, that's a good ghost—go on. (PETERS, *mad all through, does as he is told, picking up the key from floor and going upstairs.)* Better sit down, boys, and make yourselves comfortable. We're liable to have quite a wait.

(MAX *sits* L. *of table.* MAGEE *goes up* R.)

HAYDEN. Well, I'll be running along.
MAGEE. *(Stops* HAYDEN *as he starts for door)* Better stay a while, Mr. Hayden; I'd like to have your wife meet you. I don't think she's ever had the pleasure.

(MYRA *and* PETERS *enter on balcony and start downstairs.)*

HAYDEN. *(Down to* CARGAN, R. *of table)* What the devil sort of a man is this?

(BLAND *knocks on door. All jump and look upstage.)*

MAGEE. Well, here's a novelty at last—a man without a key.
HAYDEN. It's Bland. I have his key; I'll let him in. *(Starts for door.)*
MAGEE. Don't bother. I have a dandy little key of my own; I'll let him in. *(Opens door, keeping all covered.* HAYDEN *goes over* R.*)*
BLAND. *(Enters as* MAGEE *unlocks door, the latter keeping him covered.* BLAND *comes down* R. *to* HAYDEN. *Men all sit as* BLAND *enters.* BLAND *to* HAYDEN) What's the matter, Guv'nor?
HAYDEN. I don't know.
BLAND. *(Goes to* MAGEE, L.C., *as he recognizes him)* That's him, the man I told you about. He locked me in!
MAGEE. Oh, hello! Are you back again? I thought you jumped out of town.
BLAND. *(Over to* CARGAN *at table—*MAGEE *goes over* R.C.*)* Did you get it all right?
CARGAN. No; he's got it.

"Seven Keys To Baldpate" *See Page 59, Act II*
MAGEE: "Two o'clock. We've been sitting here over twenty minutes already. I think someone ought to say something. Let's start a conversation, things are getting awfully dull."
Left to Right: Myra Thornhill, Wm. Hallowell Magee, John Bland, Thomas Hayden, Jim Cargan, Peters, Lou Max

BLAND. What? *(Rushes over to* MAGEE.) Give me that money!

MAGEE. *(Covering* BLAND *with gun)* Say, I killed a man once for hollering at me. (BLAND *backs away to* L. PETERS *comes downstairs to* L. *above table. To* MYRA, *as she advances slowly to* C.) Ah, here we are! Mr. Hayden, although I think you are getting a shade the best of it, this young lady claims to be your wife.

HAYDEN. What! *(Over to* MYRA, C.) You claim what?

MYRA. Go on, holler your head off, grandpa! *(As she strolls languidly over* R. *to fireplace.)* It's music to my ears to hear an old guy squawk. *(Sits in chair in front of fire.* HAYDEN *goes to* BLAND, L.C.)

BLAND. *(Waves* HAYDEN *away.* HAYDEN *goes upstage.* BLAND *crosses to* MAGEE, R.C.) What are you going to do with that money?

MAGEE. *(Goes up around* BLAND *and up* R.C., *keeping all covered)* I haven't got the money. *(All turn and look at him in amazement.)* It's on its way to Reuton. Miss Norton will see that it is placed in safe and proper hands directly she arrives at the office of the "Reuton Daily Star."

CARGAN. The "Daily Star!" We're gone! *(To* MAGEE) Where did Mrs. Rhodes go?

MAGEE. Out of your life forever, Cargan; she's got your number. (CARGAN *lowers his head without speaking. Pause, then* MAGEE *gets chair for* BLAND *and places it* R.C.) Sit down there. (BLAND *pays no attention.)* Did you hear me? Sit! (BLAND *sits slowly and sulkily.)* Sit down, Hermy. Come on, that's a nice ghost, go on. (PETERS *sits above table.* MAGEE *places chair for* HAYDEN.) Sit down, Hayden.

HAYDEN. I don't care to sit down, sir.

MAGEE. Do as you're told; sit down.

HAYDEN. Confound it, sir, do you know that I'm

the president of the Reuton-Asquewan Railway Company?

MAGEE. I wouldn't care if you were president of the National League. Sit down! (HAYDEN *sits, indignant*. MAGEE *sits in chair, front of switchboard, facing all and covering them with gun.*) Now we're all going to stay right here till that 'phone bell rings and I get word that Miss Norton is safe and sound in Reuton. That may mean three hours or it may mean six hours; but we're all going to stay right here together, no matter how long it takes; so get comfortable and sit as easy as you can. (*All move uneasily.*)

CARGAN. (*To* MAX, *after a pause*) So you tried to cross me, eh? The chances are I'll kill you for this.

BLAND. (*After a pause, looking at* HAYDEN) I'm afraid I made a mistake in bringing you up here, Guv'nor.

HAYDEN. (*After a slight pause*) You're always making mistakes, you damned blockheaded fool!

MAX. (*After a pause*) I'm sorry I got you into this, Myra. (*No reply from her.*) Oh, Myra, I say I'm sorry I got you into this.

MYRA. (*Turns and looks at* MAX) Oh, go to hell!

PETERS. (*After a slight pause*) I hope to God you're all sent to prison for life!

MAGEE. (*After a pause*) This is going to be a nice, pleasant little party; I can see that right now. (*After three counts, ring curtain.*)

SLOW CURTAIN

ACT II

The curtain rises on the same situation.
After curtain is up, there is silence for about six seconds, then the clock is heard striking Two.
HAYDEN *takes out his watch and looks at it.* ALL *squirm and look at each other impatiently.*

MAGEE. Two o'clock. We've been sitting here over twenty minutes already. Say, Hermy, you'd better put another log on the fire. (PETERS *crosses to fireplace, puts a log on the fire, looks closely at* MYRA *in front of fireplace, then goes back to former position and sits.*) I think someone ought to say something. Come on, let's start a conversation. Things are getting awfully dull.
HAYDEN. *(Gets up after a short pause and goes toward* MAGEE) This is all damned nonsense! I refuse to stay here another minute.
MAGEE. *(Coolly, and without moving)* Sit down, Hayden. I'm very sorry to inconvenience you in this way, but it's necessary that you should stay here and keep us company; so sit down before I shoot you down! That's a good little president. (HAYDEN *sits sulkily.*) That's it. Now, let me see, what can we talk about to kill the monotony and keep things sort of lively? I have it! Let's all tell each other where we got our keys to Baldpate. *(All move uneasily.)* What do you think of the idea? *(No reply.)* No? Well, I'll start the ball rolling, then perhaps we'll all 'fess up. I brought a letter from the man who owns the inn to the caretaker, giving him instructions to turn the key over to me. That's

how I got mine. Next? *(Pause. No one speaks.)* No? Big secrets, eh? *(Laughs.)* By George! that's funny. Let's see, how many keys are there? I had the first, Bland the second, Miss Norton the third, our friend the ghost the fourth, this young lady had the fifth, and, if I'm not mistaken, you had the sixth key, Mr. Cargan. Hayden doesn't count—he had Bland's key. Six keys to Baldpate so far. I wonder if there are any more.

PETERS. *(After a pause)* There are seven keys to Baldpate. *(All turn and look at* PETERS *in surprise.)*

MAGEE. Seven! How do you know?

PETERS. The old man told me the day before he died. Mine's the original—all the others are imitations. *(All turn from him in disgust.)*

MAGEE. Seven keys, eh? *More* company expected. More melodrama, I suppose. Where did you get your key, Bland?

BLAND *and* MAGEE. *(Together)* None of your damned business!

MAGEE. *(Laughs)* I knew you were going to say that. How about you, Mr. Cargan? Perhaps you'll be good enough to throw some light on the key subject. Where did you get yours?

CARGAN. I wouldn't tell you if my life was at stake.

MAGEE. Well, perhaps the young lady will be good enough to inform me where her key came from? *(All turn and look at* MYRA.*)*

MYRA. *(Turns and faces men)* I've no objections.

MAX. *(Pleadingly)* Myra, please!

MYRA. *(Pointing to* MAX*)* He gave the key to me. *(All turn and look at* MAX.*)*

CARGAN. *(To* MAX*)* Where did you get a key to Baldpate?

MAX. I can't tell you, Mr. Mayor; I've sworn never to tell.

CARGAN. *(To* MYRA*)* I suppose he also gave you the combination to the safe.

MYRA. He did.

MAX. *(Pleadingly)* Myra!

MYRA. Oh, shut up! You never were anything but a cry baby! You've got me into a pretty mess! Do you think I'm going to sit here like a fool and not pay you back when I've got the chance to do it? *(Gets up and faces men. They all stare at her.)* I'll tell you the whole scheme. I was to come here and make off with the package, and Cargan was to follow and find it gone. We were to meet to-morrow and divide the money equally.

CARGAN. *(Turns on* MAX*)* You rat! *(*MAX *turns from* CARGAN *in hangdog fashion.)*

MYRA. His excuse to Cargan for the disappearance of the money was going to be to accuse Bland of never having put it there. *(Points to* BLAND *at mention of his name.)*

BLAND. What! *(Starts toward* L.*)*

MAGEE. Sit down, Bland. *(*BLAND *hesitates, then sits.)*

BLAND. *(Turning to* HAYDEN*)* Do you hear that, Guv'nor? He was going to accuse me of stealing the money.

CARGAN. *(To* MAX*)* You mark my words, I'm going to kill you for this!

BLAND. *(To* CARGAN*)* Where did you get a key to Baldpate, Cargan? You told me you couldn't get in here unless I met you and unlocked the door.

*(*CARGAN *looks embarrassed, but does not reply.)*

MYRA. I can explain that. *(All look toward her.)* He was to meet you here to-morrow morning at nine o'clock. Am I right?

BLAND. That's right; I made the appointment over the 'phone.

MYRA. Well, the plan was to steal in here in the dead of night and take the money. He fully intended to keep his appointment here to-morrow morning, however, and appear just as much surprised as you would have been when you discovered the safe empty and the package gone. In other words, he was going to cross not only you, but Hayden and everyone else connected with the bribe. He tried to cross you—*(Points to* BLAND.)—and Lou Max tried to double cross him. *(Points to* CARGAN. *Laughs and sits.)* If I hadn't been interrupted by our friend here—*(Nods her head in* MAGEE's *direction)*—I'd have gotten the money and *triple* crossed the whole outfit!

BLAND *and* HAYDEN. What!

MYRA. Yes, that was my intention. Scruples are a joke when one is dealing with crooks?

CARGAN. *(Starts up)* Who's a crook?

MAGEE. Sit down, Cargan.

CARGAN. *(Infuriated)* Do you think I'll stand to be——

MAGEE. *(Sternly)* Sit down, I tell you! I'm the school-teacher here. Be a good little mayor and sit down. (CARGAN *sits.)*

MYRA. *(Sneeringly, after a slight pause)* Why, you're not even clever crooks. You trusted Max, and Max trusted me. *(Laughs.)* A fine chance either one of you had if ever I had gotten hold of that money!

HAYDEN. *(To* BLAND, *after thinking a moment)* Who is this woman?

BLAND. I don't know.

CARGAN. *(Turns to* HAYDEN) Her name is Thornhill. Don't believe a word she says, Hayden; her oath isn't worth a nickel. She's a professional blackmailer, pure and simple.

HAYDEN. *(To* MYRA) Is this true?
MYRA. I never heard of a pure and simple blackmailer, did you? *(Laughs.)* So far as my word is concerned, I fancy it will carry as much weight as the word of a crooked politician or the word of his man "Friday," whom he knows to be an ex-convict.
MAX. *(Starts up)* What!
MAGEE. Sit down, Maxy; it's just getting good. (MAX *slinks into his chair.)*
HAYDEN. *(To* BLAND, *who looks at him)* Fine people you've introduced me to, you lunk-headed idiot!
BLAND. Well, what are you blaming me for? You wanted the deal put through, didn't you? After this you can do your own crooked work. I'm not anxious to get mixed up in a thing of this kind. You've got a fine nerve to go after me.
HAYDEN. *(Gets up)* How dare you talk to your employer in such a manner!
BLAND. Oh, sit down! (HAYDEN *sits.)* What do you think I care for this job? I told you to stay out of the deal—that it was wrong. You know well enough that it's only cheating the city of Reuton out of its rights. If this thing ever comes to light, we're all lucky if we don't spend five or six years in a stone yard! I tell you right now, if it comes to a show-down, I'm going to make a clean breast of the whole affair. I don't care who I send away, so long as I can save myself. You needn't think you can get me in a fix like this and have me keep my mouth shut. No, sir; I'm going to tell the truth, and I don't care a damn who suffers, so long as I get away.
MYRA. *(Laughs)* One of our best little squealers!
BLAND. *(To* MYRA) Well. you squealed, didn't you?
MYRA. Sure, I'm with you, Cutey! I'm going to

scream my head off all over the place. *(All show alarm.)*

CARGAN. *(To* MAX, *after a pause)* So you tried to cross me, eh?

MAX. Certainly I tried to cross you. Why shouldn't I? You're around crossing everybody, ain't you? *(Rises.)* I've stood for your loud talk long enough, Cargan. I've been wanting to call you for the last two years. You're a great big bluff, that's all you are, and I'm going to get even for that punch you took at me, do you hear? Now you shoot any more of that killing stuff at me, and I'll go after you like a wild bear! You're never going to kill anybody, you haven't got the nerve; but I have, and the next bluff you make at me will be your last! *(Sits.)* It's your fault I'm mixed up in this affair, and the best thing you can do is to get me away clean, do you understand? *(Smashes table with fist. Pause, then looks at* HAYDEN.) You didn't think you were going to get that franchise for two hundred thousand, did you, Hayden? Why, this man would have bled you for half a million before the bill went through, and then held you up for hush money besides. I know what I'm talking about. He was going to rob you, Hayden, and I dare him to call me a liar! *(All look at* CARGAN, *who swallows the insult in fear of* MAX's *attitude.)*

HAYDEN. *(After a pause)* Cargan, is it true that you were going to rob me of this money?

CARGAN. *(Turns to* HAYDEN, *after a slight pause)* Well, if you want to know—yes, that's what I was going to do, rob you; just what you deserve. You were trying to rob the city, weren't you? You're just as much a thief as I am. If I'm a crook, it's your kind that has made me so—you, with your rotten money, tempting men to lie and steal! *(Settles back in his chair.)* Big corporations such as yours are the cause of corrupt politics in this country, and mean it, I tell you! I'm innocent! Why, I wouldn't harm a fly!

HAYDEN. *(Goes* R.C. *to* MAX *and silences him roughly)* Keep quiet, you damn fool! Do you want the world to hear you?

(MAGEE *resumes pounding on the door. Just as* BLAND *and* CARGAN *get to first landing,* MAGEE *kicks the door open from the inside, and in the breakaway the lock falls to the floor.* MAGEE *enters on balcony as the door flies open,* PETERS *following him out.* MAGEE *comes to first landing and follows* BLAND *and* CARGAN *up opposite stairs a few steps.* PETERS *remains outside door* R. BLAND *and* CARGAN *stop only a second on first landing, and then continue on up the stairs during following lines.)*

MAGEE. What's happened?
CARGAN. She's fainted, that's all.
MAGEE. Where are you taking her?
CARGAN. You'll keep out of this, young fellow, if you know what's good for you! (BLAND *and* CARGAN *exit into room* R., CARGAN *closing door.)*

MAGEE. *(Has followed them on balcony. Watches them exit with* MYRA, *then rushes downstairs to* HAYDEN C.) Who fired that pistol shot?
MAX. (R.—*blurts out)* It was an accident!
HAYDEN. *(Quickly to* MAX, R.C.) Shut up!
MAGEE. See here, Hayden, if there's anything wrong here, you can't afford to mix up in it; you're too big a man.
MAX. *(Hysterically)* I didn't mean to kill her. I'm not responsible! It was an accident.
MAGEE. (R.C.) Oh, we have a murder case on our hands—is that the idea?
HAYDEN. (R. *of* MAGEE) I don't know; but what-

you're just the kind of a sneak that helps build prisons that are filled with the poor devils that do your dirty work. You're worse than a crook—you're a maker of crooks. *(Turns to* HAYDEN, *leans forward and points at him.)* But I promise you, Hayden, that if I go up for this, you'll go with me! It's your fault that I entered into this thing, and, by Gad! I'll get even if I have to lie over a Bible and swear your life away! *(Turns, facing audience.)* Rob you! Humph! You've got a hell of a gall to yell about being robbed, you have!

PETERS. *(After slight pause)* I hope the prison catches fire and you're all burned to a crisp!

MAGEE. *(Laughs)* You know, my suggestion was to start a conversation, not a rough house.

HAYDEN. *(After a slight pause)* This woman who took the money—who is she?

MYRA. A newspaper reporter.

BLAND. On the "Daily Star."

CARGAN. The sheet that has fought me ever since I've been in office. They've got me this time, sure!

MAX. *(After a pause, looking nervously at* MAGEE*)* How much longer are you going to keep us here?

MAGEE. That's for the telephone to say. I'll release you as soon as I'm sure Miss Norton is safe and sound in Reuton. *(All turn toward* MAGEE, *surprised.)*

BLAND. Then you're not going to turn us over to the police?

MAGEE. Certainly not. Why should I? *(Movement of relief from all.)*

PETERS. *(Gets up)* Because they're a lot of crooks. *(All turn toward* PETERS.*)* Oh, how I'd love to be on the jury!

MAGEE. Sit down, Hermy. I need a little target practise, and remember, there's no law against killing ghosts! *(*PETERS *sits.)*

HAYDEN. There's no train to Reuton till five o'clock. That means we must stay here till six, eh?

MAGEE. I'm afraid so, unless they make it by automobile from Asquewan. It means several hours at the best, so you might as well be patient; you've got a long wait. *(All move uneasily.)*

MYRA. *(Cuddling up in her chair)* Me for my beauty sleep! Good-night. *(Short pause, then 'phone rings. All start and stare at it.* MAGEE *gets up and stops buzzer.)*

MAX. She couldn't have made it as quick as that. It's over an hour by automobile.

MAGEE. *(Keeps them all covered with gun)* Answer that 'phone, please, Miss Thornhill. (MYRA *gets up and goes to 'phone.* MAGEE *backs upstage.)* I'm going to keep looking straight ahead of me tonight. Hurry, please. Give me the message as you get it. I'll tell you what to say if it requires an answer.

MYRA. *(At 'phone, in a bored tone)* Hello! . . . Yes, Baldpate Inn. . . . Yes, I know who you mean. Just a moment. *(To* MAGEE*)* Someone wants to talk to you.

MAGEE. Get the name.

MYRA. *(In 'phone)* Hello! who is this, please? . . . Oh, yes. . . . Very well, I'll tell him. *(Turns to* MAGEE.*)* Miss Norton.

MAGEE. Say that it is impossible for me to turn my back long enough to come to the 'phone, and that you will take the message and repeat it to me as you get it.

MYRA. *(In 'phone.* MAGEE *backs up* R.C.*)* It is impossible for him to turn his back long enough to come to the 'phone. You are to give me the message and I am to repeat it to him as I get it. . . . You're talking from the Commercial House in Asquewan. . . . You missed the package of money five minutes ago. . . *(All turn.)* You either dropped it in the inn before you left, or else lost it while hurrying down the mountain. . . . Search the inn thoroughly. *(Pause, while all look around room.)* Ask him whether or not you should notify the police. *(All show fear.)* You're nearly crazy, and don't know which way to turn. . . . Just a moment. *(Turns and looks at* MAGEE.) Well, what shall I say?

MAGEE. *(Looks around at all, then answers, after a pause)* Say to hold the wire.

MYRA. *(In 'phone)* Hold the wire, please. *(Gets up and goes toward chair* R.*)*

HAYDEN. The money lost!

CARGAN. Thank God, there goes their evidence!

MAX. Who ever heard of losing two hundred thousand dollars!

BLAND. Can't be done outside of Wall Street. Surest thing you know, she's holding out.

MAGEE. *(Smiles)* You're a quick thinker, Miss Thornhill.

MYRA. *(Turns to* MAGEE*)* What do you mean?

MAGEE. That I don't believe you got that message at all.

MYRA. *(Shrugs her shoulders indifferently)* Very well; she's on the wire—see for yourself. *(Sits in chair in front of fire.)*

MAGEE. Come here, Hermy.

PETERS. My name's not Henry; my name's Peters.

MAGEE. Well, whatever it is, come here. (PETERS *goes up to* MAGEE, *up* R.) I know you don't like anybody in this room any better than I do, so I'm going to take a chance on you. Take this gun and guard that door until I get this message, and you kill the first man or woman that makes a move, do you understand?

PETERS. *(Vindictively)* I'd like to kill them all!

MAGEE. Don't shoot unless you have to. *(He hands* PETERS *the gun and goes to 'phone.)* Hello!

PETERS. Damn you, Cargan, I've got you at last!

(PETERS *goes toward* CARGAN *and is grabbed by* HAYDEN. MYRA *screams and jumps up.* BLAND *springs on* MAGEE *and struggles with him.* MAX *rushes over to* R., *and the two overpower* MAGEE *at 'phone. When* HAYDEN *grabs* PETERS, CARGAN *rushes over and struggles with* PETERS, *wrestling gun from him.)*

MAX. *(To* MAGEE) Take it easy, young fellow; you haven't got a chance.
BLAND. We've got him!
CARGAN. *(After wrenching gun from* PETERS, *he hits him a blow, knocking him down)* What do you think of that? (BLAND *and* MAX *are* R., *each holding* MAGEE *by the arms.* PETERS *is on the floor* C., CARGAN *standing over him, with gun.* HAYDEN *is* L., *looking on.* CARGAN *to* PETERS) So you wanted to take a shot at me, eh? *(Kicks* PETERS.) Get up! (PETERS *gets up in fear.* CARGAN *backs upstage slightly.)* Put them both up in the room where he put us, and lock the door.
BLAND. They can make a getaway from the window, Cargan; I did it myself.
CARGAN. There's no window in that room; it's a linen closet. Put them up there. *(He backs upstage, gun in hand.* PETERS *starts upstairs.)*
MAGEE. *(To* CARGAN, *as he comes to* C. *on way to stairs)* What's the idea, Cargan?
CARGAN. *(Backing up* C. *and pointing gun)* Go on, I'm the school-teacher now—do as you're told. (HAYDEN *goes to extreme* L. *as* PETERS *and* MAGEE *go upstairs, followed by* MAX. BLAND *goes* R., *below 'phone.* CARGAN *speaks next lines to* MYRA *with his back to her.)* Get on that 'phone, Miss Thornhill, and tell that woman not to notify the police. Say

SEVEN KEYS TO BALDPATE 69

that she is to return here at once, and see what she says.

(MYRA *goes to 'phone.* MAGEE *and* MAX *are now on landing.* PETERS *is standing at door of room* L. *on balcony.*)

MYRA. *(In 'phone)* Hello! . . . Yes. . . . Why, the message is that you are not to notify the police of the loss. Say nothing to anyone, but return here at once. . . . That is the message. . . . Yes, good-bye. *(Hangs up receiver.)*
CARGAN. *(To* MYRA, *still watching* MAGEE) All right.
MYRA. *(Rising from switchboard)* As quick as she can get here, she says. *(Goes down* R. *to chair.)*
MAGEE. *(Stops on landing as he hears 'phone conversation)* What are you going to do, Cargan?
CARGAN. Never mind; I'm running things now. Get in there! (PETERS *exits into room* L. *on balcony.)*
MAGEE. You harm that girl, and I'll get you if it's the last act of my life!
CARGAN. I've read that kind of talk in books.
MAGEE. I write books of that kind, but I'm talking real talk now!
MAX. *(To* MAGEE) Go on, get in there.

(MAGEE *goes upstairs and exits into room* L. MAX *locks door and comes to foot of stairs.* BLAND *has gone* L. CARGAN *puts gun in his pocket and comes down* C.*)*

HAYDEN. *(Over to* CARGAN *at* C.) Now what's the move, Cargan?
CARGAN. We're going to get that money if she's got it on her.
BLAND. You don't think she's fool enough to

bring it back with her if she's trying to get away with it, do you?

HAYDEN. What are you going to do with it if you find it on her, Cargan?

CARGAN. Keep it, of course.

HAYDEN. It's my money.

CARGAN. Our agreement holds good. You people will get the franchise. Don't worry.

HAYDEN. Why, you've just openly declared that you were going to rob me of the money.

CARGAN. Oh, because I was mad clean through. Wasn't I being accused right and left? I didn't mean a word I said, Hayden. I don't even know now what I said. *(Pats* HAYDEN *ingratiatingly on the shoulders, then goes up* C., *looking up at room* L.*)*

HAYDEN. *(Goes to* BLAND, *who is below table* L.*)* What do you think, Bland?

(CARGAN *and* MAX *come downstage to* C.*)*

BLAND. Don't ask me; you bawled me out once to-night; that's enough!

CARGAN. I haven't forgotten what you said to me, Mr. Max.

MAX. I don't want you to forget it. I want you to remember it all your life. *(As* CARGAN *reaches for gun.)* I wouldn't care if you had six guns on you. Cut out that wild talk; I ain't going to listen to it any more. Why, you're nothing but a cheap coward, Cargan! (CARGAN *looks at* MAX *a moment, then turns upstage, cowed.* MAX *crosses to* MYRA, R.*)* So you tried to double cross me, eh?

MYRA. *(Turns and faces* MAX) Why, certainly! Who are you?

MAX. Why, damn you, I—— *(Raises his hand to strike* MYRA, *who shrinks away.)*

BLAND. *(Crossing quickly to* C.*)* Here, wait a minute, Max; nothing like that while I'm around.

MAX. *(Turns to* BLAND*)* Maybe you want some of it? Why, I—— *(Raises his hand to strike* BLAND.*)*

BLAND. *(Grabs* MAX'S *arm and throws it back)* Now behave yourself. The same speech you just made to Cargan goes for me. I want you to cut out this wild talk. I'm not going to listen to any more of it. I'll put you on your back if you make another bluff at me!

HAYDEN. *(Goes toward* MAX *and* BLAND, C*)* Gentlemen, gentlemen, please! *(*MAX *and* BLAND *look each other in the eye for a moment, then* MAX *goes up* R.*, near safe.)*

BLAND. *(Turns to* HAYDEN *after* MAX *has gone up* R.*)* You keep out of this, Hayden; you'll get all you're looking for if you don't. *(Raises his hand to* HAYDEN *as if to strike.)*

HAYDEN. Put it down! Put it down, do you hear me? What do you mean by raising your hand to me? Why, damn me, for two pins I'd take and wipe up the floor with you! I can whip a whole army of cowards like you! Now get away from me! Get away from me before I knock you down! *(*BLAND, *surprised at* HAYDEN'S *attitude, goes up to* C. *door, after staring at* HAYDEN *a moment.* HAYDEN *goes to* MYRA R. MAX *goes to safe and begins working combination.)* Now, Madam, what do you mean by claiming to be my wife? I demand an explanation.

MYRA. *(Turns quickly and angrily on* HAYDEN*)* Now let me tell you something, old man. You can scare these three little boys, but I don't want you to annoy me, because I've got a nasty temper; so go on, get away before I lose it!

*(*HAYDEN *stares at* MYRA, *dumbfounded, then goes*

quickly to L. MYRA *seats herself in chair after* HAYDEN *turns from her.* MAX, *by this time, has worked combination of safe, and at this point the door flies open. He grabs a gun from safe and slams door shut.* CARGAN, *who has been standing at foot of stairs looking up at room* L., *turns quickly as he hears the door slam and crosses quickly to* R.C., *catching* MAX *at safe door.* BLAND *crosses* CARGAN *to* L.C.)

CARGAN. *(Pulling his gun)* Get away from that safe! What are you doing there?

MAX. *(Flashes revolver.* MYRA *rises and stands* L. *of chair and below it)* Oh, you needn't be afraid. I ain't going to do anything, only I—— (MAX *has come in front of desk while speaking above lines, and now takes deliberate aim at* MYRA *and shoots. She screams and drops into chair.)*

BLAND. *(Runs to* MYRA) God!

CARGAN. *(Crosses to* L. *of* MAX) What's the matter, Max? Have you gone crazy? *(Puts gun in his pocket.)*

HAYDEN. *(Over to* R. *of* MAX, *looking toward* MYRA) Now we're in for it. Is she hurt?

MAX. *(Down* L. *of* HAYDEN) I couldn't help it; it was an accident! I didn't mean it, I tell you!

(MAGEE *raps on door upstairs. All look up.)*

MAGEE. *(From upstairs)* What's wrong down there? *(Raps again.)* What's happened? *(All stand rigid, staring.)*

BLAND. *(In a low voice)* Put out the lights.

(CARGAN *tiptoes upstage and turns out bracket lights, leaving only the reflection of burning logs on* MYRA'S *face, then tiptoes back to* C.)

"SEVEN KEYS TO BALDPATE." MAX: "Take it easy, young fellow, you haven't got a chance." See Page 68, Act II
Left to Right: Myra Thornhill, John Bland, Wm. H. Magee, Lou Max, Jim Cargan, Peters, Thomas Hayden

HAYDEN. Anything serious, Bland?
BLAND. You're a damn good shot, Max; you got her, all right! *(Is feeling* MYRA's *pulse.)*
CARGAN. Don't say that! *(Backs away to* L.C.*)*
HAYDEN. It can't be possible!
BLAND. It's all over—she's gone! *(Drops her hand, then turns her chair around to* R.*)*
MAX. *(*R.C.*, wild-eyed)* But I didn't mean it, I tell you—it was an accident!
BLAND. You lie!
CARGAN. I saw you take aim.
HAYDEN. So did I.
MAX. *(Pleadingly)* No, no, don't say that! It isn't so! Before Heaven, I swear it was an accident!

(MAGEE *pounds on door upstairs.)*

HAYDEN, CARGAN *and* BLAND. *(To* MAX. HAYDEN *is* L. *of* MAX*)* Ssh! *(All look up in direction of door.)*
MAGEE. *(From room* R.*)* Tell me what the matter is down there.
CARGAN. *(Goes to foot of stairs and calls up)* Everything's all right—nothing wrong.
MAGEE. I know better! Open this door! *(Pounds on door.)*
BLAND. Give me a hand, Cargan, and we'll get her out of here. (MAX *and* HAYDEN *go up* C.*)*
CARGAN. *(Over to* BLAND*)* Where do you mean?
BLAND. *(Pointing to room* R. *on balcony)* Up in that room. Come on, hurry up! (CARGAN *assists* BLAND *in lifting* MYRA *to the latter's shoulders.* BLAND *starts for stairs, carrying* MYRA; CARGAN *following with her wraps, etc.)*
MAX. *(*R.C. *as* BLAND *passes with* MYRA*)* I didn't

ever it is, we're all in this thing together. We must frame a story and stick to it, do you understand?

MAGEE. No, I don't understand.

HAYDEN. We must claim suicide.

MAX. (*Going toward* C.—HAYDEN *goes up* C.) That's it! She killed herself! I was an eye-witness —she killed herself!

MAGEE. Do you think I'd enter into such a dastardly scheme? (BLAND *and* CARGAN *enter and stand on balcony* C., *listening.*) No! If it's murder, there's the murderer—*(Points to* MAX, *crosses to him* R., *then back to* L.C.*)*—self-confessed. But you're all as guilty as this man—every one of you. It's the outcome and result of rotten politics and greed. I'll swear to every word that's been uttered here tonight. I've had my ear against the crack of that door for the last five minutes. I overheard every word that passed between you. I'll tell the story straight from the shoulder. You can't crawl out of it, gentlemen, with your suicide alibi. It's murder in the first degree, and I'm going to help make you pay the penalty!

(HAYDEN *and* MAX *stand staring at him.* HAYDEN *goes up* R., *near desk.* CARGAN *and* BLAND, *after a bit of pantomime, come downstairs,* CARGAN *goes to* L. *of* MAGEE *and* BLAND *to* R. *of him.* MAX *is* R.)

CARGAN. (*After a pause*—L. *of* MAGEE) I'm afraid you're in wrong here, young fellow.

(PETERS *sneaks across balcony to* R. *of it and stands listening to next few speeches, hidden behind post* R.)

CARGAN. I'm sorry for you. From the bottom of my heart I pity you. (*Takes stage a little* L. MA-

GEE *does not reply; simply looks at* CARGAN, *then at* BLAND.)

BLAND. *(After a pause)* She's dead—you killed her, all right!

(MAGEE *looks* BLAND *in the eye, then at* CARGAN. *The latter turns upstage after a pause, then crosses down to back of chair* L. MAGEE *crosses to* HAYDEN, *who comes down* C.)

HAYDEN. *(Comes down* C. *to* R. *of* MAGEE) Better plead insanity, old man; it's the only chance you've got.

(MAGEE *stares at* HAYDEN, *then crosses over to* R. *and looks* MAX *straight in the eye.* MAX *stares back at him.)*

MAX. *(After a pause)* Bad business, this carrying guns. Who was the woman—your wife?

(PETERS *exits into room on balcony* R., *closing door.* BLAND *is* L.C.)

MAGEE. *(Turns, sees the three staring at him, smiles and comes* C.) No, no, gentlemen! You can't get away with it! It's good melodrama, but it's old stuff. I know every trick of the trade. I've written it by the yard. You can't intimidate me. I won't be third-degreed. You work very well together, but it's rough work, and it isn't going to get you anything. Besides, you forget I have a witness in Peters, the hermit. *(All turn and look up at room* L.)

CARGAN. *(Front of table* L.—*looks up at room, then says to* BLAND) Get him. Bring him down. *(Goes to foot of stairs as* BLAND *goes upstairs.)*

BLAND. *(Runs up and looks into room L., then comes out on balcony)* He's gone!

(HAYDEN *looks at* MAX, *then back to* BLAND.)

CARGAN. Gone! Where?
BLAND. *(Comes quickly down the stairs)* He probably found a way; he knows the place better than we do. *(Goes R. of* MAGEE.*)*
CARGAN. *(Comes down to* MAGEE, R.C.*)* I saw you when you fired; you shot to kill.
BLAND. *(R. of* MAGEE*)* I tried to knock the gun from your hand, but I was too late. *(Goes upstage.)*
HAYDEN. *(R. of* BLAND*)* I didn't witness the shooting myself, but I turned just in time to grab you before you got away.
MAX. *(R.)* But you shouldn't have choked her; that was the brutal part of it.
MAGEE. *(Starts for* MAX, *who backs away to fireplace, frightened)* Why, you dog, I——

(CHIEF KENNEDY *appears outside door and pounds on it three times. All on stage stop abruptly and look toward door, holding the picture for a repeat of the pounding.*)

CARGAN. *(Loudly)* Who's there?
KENNEDY. *(Yells through door from outside)* Open this door in the name of the law!
(WARN Lights.)
MAX. The police!
HAYDEN. *(Quickly to* MAX*)* Keep quiet! *(Gets behind desk.)*
BLAND. *(To* CARGAN*)* You'd better let them in, Cargan.
MAGEE. *(Starts for door)* I'll unlock the door.
CARGAN. No, you don't; I'll attend to it!

(*Crosses* MAGEE, *goes up to door and unlocks it.* KENNEDY *steps in, watching* CARGAN *as the latter locks the door. As* CARGAN *is about to put key in his pocket,* KENNEDY *speaks.* BLAND *has gone* L., *above table, when* CARGAN *goes up to door.)*

KENNEDY. (*Up* L.C., *just inside door*) Here, wait a minute! I'll take that key. I'll take that gun I saw you stick in your pocket, too.

BLAND. (*Takes a couple of steps toward* KENNEDY *up* L.) What authority have you?

KENNEDY. (*Comes down* L.C. *to* BLAND) Close your trap! I'm Chief Kennedy of the Asquewan Falls Police Headquarters—that's my authority!

CARGAN. (*Down to* KENNEDY, *pointing to* BLAND) It's all right, Chief; he's all right.

KENNEDY. Where's the light switch?

MAGEE. Up there to your left.

KENNEDY. (*Goes up* L. *of door and turns on lights, then comes downstage* L. *of* CARGAN, *recognizing him*) Hello, Mr. Mayor! What are you doing here?

CARGAN. I can explain all that.

MAGEE. (*Pointing to* MAX) That man has a gun on him also. (HAYDEN *moves over toward* L. *slowly.*)

KENNEDY. (*Goes over* R.C. *and looks* MAGEE *over carefully*) Who are you? (CARGAN *crosses to* L.C.)

MAGEE. I'll tell you who I am at the proper time and place. You'd better get on your job quick here, Chief; there's something doing. Two of these men are carrying weapons, and two of them also have keys to that door. I'm telling you this to prevent a getaway.

KENNEDY. What are you trying to do, run the police department?

MAGEE. This is an important case, Chief. Thousands of dollars are involved, and a crime committed besides. I advise placing every man in this room under arrest immediately.

KENNEDY. *(To* CARGAN*)* What's this all about, Mr. Mayor? *(All appear anxious.)*

CARGAN. He's four-flushing, Chief. He's stalling for a chance to break away.

KENNEDY. Don't be afraid; I've got men outside; nobody'll get away. *(Crosses* MAGEE *to* MAX R., *and looks at him closely.)* Lou Max, eh? Quite a crowd of celebrities. *(To* MAX*)* You got a gun? (MAX *hands him his gun.)* What are you totin' this for? *(No reply from* MAX. CHIEF *turns and fans* MAGEE.*)* He's clean. *(Turns* MAGEE *upstage and crosses to* CARGAN.*)* I'm sorry to trouble you, Mr. Mayor, but I'll have to relieve you of that hardware. (CARGAN *hands* CHIEF *his gun.)* And the key, too, please. (CARGAN *hands* CHIEF *his key.)* I've come here to investigate, and I've got to do my duty. *(Crosses* CARGAN *over to* BLAND L.C.*)*

BLAND. *(Holding up his hands as* CHIEF *approaches him)* There's nothing on me.

KENNEDY. *(Fans* BLAND*)* Who's got the other key? He said there were two.

BLAND. *(Points to* HAYDEN*)* This gentleman.

KENNEDY. *(Goes to* HAYDEN L., *who hands the* CHIEF *his key)* Hello! Mr. Hayden. Humph! This is a real highbrow affair, isn't it? Well—— *(Smiles, goes up* C. *to* R. *of* CARGAN *and looks them all over.)* Come on, somebody open up. What's the big gathering all about?

MAX. *(Pointing to* MAGEE*)* He's got a key. Make him give it up.

KENNEDY. *(To* MAGEE*)* Come on. (MAGEE *hands* CHIEF *his key.)* You got anything more to say?

MAGEE. I prefer to tell my story in the presence of witnesses. I insist upon the immediate arrest of everyone here, myself included.

HAYDEN. Don't mind him, Chief; he's a madman.

KENNEDY. Well, somebody telephoned police headquarters from here about two hours ago, and when we got on the wire Central said they'd hung up. We got a new connection, and asked if they'd called, and some woman said, "No, it was a mistake." We got to thinking it over at headquarters, and it didn't listen good, so we looked it up and found out that the call had been put in from Baldpate Inn; so I made up my mind to come here and investigate. Now, when I started up the mountain ten minutes ago the lights were on full blast, and all of a sudden they went out, and there was a pistol shot, too. Every one of my men heard the report, and we all agree it came from this direction. Now, what's it all about?

MAGEE. 'Twas I who called up police headquarters. *(All look at* MAGEE.*)*

KENNEDY. You! The Sergeant said it was a woman's voice on the wire.

MAGEE. That was the second time when you called up, but I tried to get you first.

KENNEDY. What for?

MAGEE. I don't intend to tell my story until I'm under oath. I want every word I say to go on the court records. I charge these men with conspiracy and murder!

KENNEDY. What is this, Cargan?

CARGAN. The poor devil's gone mad, I guess. He shot and killed a woman a few minutes ago, and he's accused every man here of the crime.

KENNEDY. Murder, eh?

HAYDEN. Yes, cold-blooded murder.

KENNEDY. *(To* MAGEE*)* Who was the woman you shot?

MAGEE. Don't let these men get away with this, Chief. I can prove my innocence. *(Pointing to*

MAX.) There's the real murderer. These men know it as well as I do. They're accusing me in an attempt to save their own necks. They're afraid to tell the truth because this man is a squealer, and they know that a confession from him of a scheme to steal the right of way for a street car franchise in Reuton will send them all to the State penitentiary. I can prove why I'm here to-night. Ask these men their reason for being here, and let's hear what they have to say.

(KENNEDY *looks from one to the other without speaking.*)

CARGAN. He's been raving like that for the last ten minutes, Chief.
KENNEDY. *(To* MAGEE) What is your reason for being here?
MAGEE. I came here to write a book.
KENNEDY. *(To* CARGAN) You're right; he's a lunatic, sure. *(To* CARGAN) Who was the woman that telephoned to headquarters?
MAGEE. Miss Norton, of the "Reuton Star."
KENNEDY. The "Reuton Star," eh? *(To* CARGAN) Is she the woman that was killed?
CARGAN. No; her name is Thornhill.
KENNEDY. Where is she?
CARGAN. In one of the rooms upstairs.
KENNEDY. Was there anybody else here besides you people?
MAGEE. Yes; Peters, the hermit.
KENNEDY. Another crazy man, eh?
BLAND. But he's disappeared.
KENNEDY. Well, he won't go far. *(Goes upstage and looks out of door.)* I've got the house surrounded. *(Coming downstage.)* I'll look the ground over before I send for the coroner. He won't be here till seven or eight o'clock. You people will

have to stay here till he comes. (CARGAN, BLAND and HAYDEN *sit near table* L. MAX *sits* R.) What room is she in? *(Looking up at balcony.)*

CARGAN. *(Gets up from table)* I'll show you, Chief. *(Starts toward stairs, leading the way, followed by the* CHIEF, HAYDEN, BLAND *and* MAX *in order named. All look back at* MAGEE *as they go upstairs.)*

KENNEDY. *(To* MAGEE, *when he gets on balcony)* Take my tip and don't try to get away, young fellow. One of those cops outside will blow your head off if you do.

MAGEE. *(Goes* L. *near foot of stairs as men go up)* You needn't be afraid. I'm going to stay right here, and I'm going to make sure these other men do until we're all taken into custody.

HAYDEN. It's a sad case, Chief.

KENNEDY. We're used to that. They generally go out of their minds after they shoot. Where is she?

CARGAN. *(Goes to door of room* R.) In here, Chief.

(CHIEF *exits into room, followed by* HAYDEN, BLAND, MAX *and* CARGAN, *the latter closing the door. During the last few speeches* PETERS *has been peering through glass in dining-room door* L. *He now enters and goes quickly to* MAGEE C.)

PETERS. I carried the body from that room through the secret passage to the cellar.

MAGEE. *(Amazed)* What!

PETERS. I heard them accuse you of the crime. *(Backs toward door* L. *slowly.)* They'll never find the secret passage—*(Laughs)*—and they'll never find the body! *(Laughs viciously.)*

MAGEE. What did you do that for, you damn fool? *(Door opens on balcony R.)*
PETERS. Hist! *(He points up at door R. on balcony.* MAGEE *looks up.* PETERS *exits hurriedly through door L.)*

(CARGAN *enters, wild-eyed, from room, runs downstairs and comes to* L.C. MAX *follows him down and goes to* R. HAYDEN *follows* MAX, *and comes down to* L.C. BLAND *follows* HAYDEN, *and comes to* R. *All the men show extreme fear.* MAGEE, *standing* C., *watches them.* KENNEDY *comes out on balcony, looks at people downstairs, then back at room for a moment, then out again at cue.)*

HAYDEN. *(To* CARGAN, *who is front of table* L.*)* What do you make of this, Cargan?
CARGAN. The damn place is haunted!
MAX. She must have escaped by the window.
BLAND. How could a dead woman jump from the window? Besides, the windows are closed.

(They all stand staring up at balcony. KENNEDY *appears from room* R. *and closes door.)*

KENNEDY. *(Comes to* C. *of balcony and stands looking down at men)* Say, what are you fellows trying to do, string me? *(Starts downstairs.)* You know I was born and brought up in New York City, even if I do live in Asquewan Falls. *(Comes down to* C. *and looks them all over.)*
HAYDEN. I can't understand it at all.
CARGAN. She was in that room ten minutes ago, Chief.
BLAND. I'll take a solemn oath on that.
MAX. My God, I'm going insane! *(Grabs chair to steady himself.)*

KENNEDY. Say, what the devil is this all about? *(Looks from one to the other.)* If you people think you can make a joke out of me, you're mistaken. I won't stand for it. Now come on, what's the answer?

MAGEE. It's no joke, Chief; there has been a murder committed here.

KENNEDY. Then where's the victim?

MAGEE. In the cellar.

BLAND, CARGAN, HAYDEN *and* MAX. What!

KENNEDY. In the cellar?

MAGEE. If I'm not mistaken, that's where she was taken after the murder.

HAYDEN. You lie!

CARGAN. You know she was taken to that room. *(Points to room* R. *on balcony.)*

BLAND. You saw us carry her there.

MAX. Of course he did.

KENNEDY. *(To* MAGEE*)* What are you trying to do, trap me in the cellar?

MAGEE. I tell you, Chief, you'll find the victim in the cellar. Then you can judge for yourself if I'm as crazy as these men claim me to be, or whether they've suddenly gone mad themselves.

KENNEDY. *(Blows his whistle)* I'll get at the bottom of this thing pretty quick! *(Rushes up to door, unlocks and opens it. Two Cops enter, come to* L. *of stage up* C. *and await orders.* KENNEDY *locks door and goes to Cops.)* Search the cellar of this place, and report to me here what you find—every nook and corner. And don't leave a thing unturned, understand? *(Cops salute.* MARY *appears outside door.)* Hurry up, then! *(Cops exit through door* L. KENNEDY *comes down* C.*)* If this thing is a practical joke, you'll all land in jail for it. I'm not going to be made the laughing stock of Asquewan Falls, I'll tell you that right now. (MARY, *who has been peering through door, opens it during this*

speech and enters. KENNEDY *turns as door opens and goes upstage.*) Hello! Who's this?
MAGEE. (*Goes* L. *as* MARY *enters*) Miss Norton! (MARY *locks door and starts down* L.C.)
KENNEDY. (*To* MARY) I'll take that key, please.
MARY. (*Hands* CHIEF *the key and goes to* MAGEE L.C.) Why are the police here?

(KENNEDY *goes down* R.C. *to* BLAND.)

MAGEE. (*Reassuring* MARY) It's all right.
KENNEDY. (*To* BLAND) Who is this woman?
BLAND. She claims to be a newspaper reporter.
MAX. She's a thief; she stole a package of money!
KENNEDY. Whose money?
HAYDEN. My money.
CARGAN. (L., *in front of table*) No, my money.
MAGEE. It's bribe money, Chief.
KENNEDY. Where is the money?
MARY. (*Turns and faces* CHIEF) The money's been lost.
BLAND, HAYDEN, MAX *and* CARGAN. What!
KENNEDY. Say, what the hell are you people trying to do to me, anyway?
MAGEE. (*To* MARY) Where did you lose it?
MARY. (*To* MAGEE—KENNEDY *goes over, listening*) I don't know—somewhere between here and Asquewan. I searched every inch of the way from the bottom of the mountain to the top. It's gone, I'm afraid.
MAGEE. Where is Mrs. Rhodes?
MARY. She became too hysterical to return. I left her at the Commercial House in Asquewan.
KENNEDY. How much money was it?
MAGEE. Two hundred thousand dollars.
KENNEDY. (*Looks from one to the other*) Come on, cut out the kidding stuff! How much was it?

HAYDEN. *(L., near table)* That's the exact amount the package contained, Chief—two hundred thousand dollars.
KENNEDY. *(To MARY)* Where'd you get this money?
MAGEE. I gave it to her.
KENNEDY. Where did you get it?
MAGEE. From Mayor Cargan.
KENNEDY. Where did you get the money, Cargan? *(No reply from CARGAN.)*
MAGEE. *(After a pause)* He took the money from that safe.
KENNEDY. *(Goes upstage a couple of steps, looks at safe, then comes back to C.)* How'd you open the safe, Cargan?
CARGAN. I didn't open the safe.
KENNEDY. Who did?
MAGEE. Peters, the hermit.
KENNEDY. Who put the money in the safe?
MAGEE. Bland. *(Points to BLAND.)* That man to your right.
KENNEDY. *(Over to BLAND, R.C.)* Where'd you get the money to put in the safe?
BLAND. From Mr. Hayden.
KENNEDY. *(Looks at HAYDEN, L.)* Is this true, Mr. Hayden?
HAYDEN. I refuse to answer for fear of incriminating myself.
KENNEDY. *(Over to MAX, R.)* What do you know about this, Max?
MAX. Don't ask me; I don't know. My brain's on fire—I'm going mad! *(Tugs at his collar, breathing hard.)*
KENNEDY. *(Comes to C. and looks them all over)* Huh! Hayden gave the money to Bland; Bland put the money in the safe; Peters opened the safe; Cargan took the money from Peters; this fellow took the money from Cargan and gave it to the news-

paper reporter; she loses the money in the mountains; then somebody killed a woman and the corpse got up and walked away,—and you expect me to believe this bunk, do you?

MARY. *(To* MAGEE) What does he mean by saying that somebody killed a woman?

MAGEE. Don't worry; it's all right. (MARY *and* MAGEE *go up* L., *near foot of stairs.)*

COP. *(Off stage)* Come on, come on! Go on, get in there! *(He opens door* L. *and throws* PETERS *to* C. *of stage. The other* COP *follows them on.)* That's all we could find in the cellar, Chief.

KENNEDY. No dead bodies or packages of money?

COP. Nothing else, Chief. *(Goes up* L. *near door.)*

KENNEDY. *(Looks at* PETERS *and laughs)* Oh, it's you, is it, Peters? So that's where you hide, eh? In the cellar of Baldpate? Well, you'll have a nice room in the county jail to-morrow.

PETERS. Damn the police; I hate them!

KENNEDY. *(Throws* PETERS *to* R.) Go on, get over there! *(To* COPS *as he goes up to door)* Guard the outside. *(As he goes up to door,* MARY *and* MAGEE *come down to* L.C. CHIEF *unlocks door. To* COPS) And question anybody who passes up or down the mountain. *(Opens door.* COPS *exit.* CHIEF *locks door and comes down stage to* MARY.) You'll have to step upstairs, Miss. I've got a lot to say to these men here, and I'm not particular about my language when I'm on a case; so come on, step upstairs.

HAYDEN. *(Extreme* L., *near table)* I don't believe this girl lost the money, Chief.

KENNEDY. Well, I'll get the matron of the jail here and have her searched. If she's got anything on her we'll get it. (MARY *starts for stairs,* CHIEF *following her up.)* Go in one of those rooms till I call you. (MARY *is now on balcony* C. CHIEF *comes downstage to* C.) Who is the woman this girl says she left at the Commercial House?

CARGAN. Mrs. Rhodes. She's all right.

BLAND. *(Goes slightly toward* CARGAN) How do we know? Maybe they're working together.

CARGAN. That's enough, Bland.

KENNEDY. *(As he goes toward 'phone all back up and watch him)* I'll call up the Commercial House and see if she's there. *(In 'phone)* Hello! Get me 35, Central, quick. (MARY *exits into room* R. *on balcony.)* Ring me when you get it. *(Hangs up receiver and comes down to* C.) What's her name again?

MAGEE. Mrs. Rhodes. (MARY *screams off stage and rushes from room to balcony.)* What's the matter?

MARY. *(Screaming)* She's dead! Someone's killed her!

ALL. Who?

MARY. *(Hysterically)* That woman there in that room! This is terrible!

(KENNEDY *looks at* MAGEE. MAGEE *looks at* CARGAN. *All stand rigid, staring at each other for a moment; then* KENNEDY, CARGAN, BLAND, HAYDEN *and* MAX *rush upstairs on balcony and cross to room* R. *As they pass in front of* MARY, *she backs up against windows and stands with arms outstretched against them.* PETERS *is standing* R., *laughing.)*

MAGEE. *(Goes over* R. *to* PETERS *quickly)* What did you do, bring her back to that room?

PETERS. Isn't that what you wanted me to do?

MAGEE. No, you blithering idiot! *(Turns and takes* MARY *in his arms as she runs to him.)*

MARY. Tell me who did this? How did it happen?

"SEVEN KEYS TO BALDPATE" MAGEE: "I've got him, get the money." *See Page 95, Act II*
Left to Right: Lou Max, Peters, Jiggs Kennedy, John Bland, Magee, Jim Cargan, Thomas Hayden, Mary Norton, Mrs. Rhodes

SEVEN KEYS TO BALDPATE 89

MAGEE. It's all right; take it easy.

(MAX, BLAND, CARGAN *and* HAYDEN *enter from room* R. *in this rotation, all wild-eyed. They line up on balcony and keep their eyes glued to door of room.* KENNEDY *enters on balcony, also keeping his eyes fixed on room. He looks at men on balcony and then down at* MAGEE *and* MARY, *who stare up at him; then at* PETERS, *who is over* R.)

KENNEDY. Say, what are you people trying to do to me? *(To men on balcony, who are still staring at door.)* Go on, get downstairs where you belong. *(Four men come downstairs and go to former positions. Telephone rings.* KENNEDY *runs downstairs.)* Don't touch that 'phone! I'll answer it! *(Looks from one to the other suspiciously.)* Is this dump haunted, or is the joke on me? *(No one replies. The 'phone still rings.)* I'll soon find out! *(Goes to 'phone. All back up and watch him.)* Hello! . . . Yes, I called you. Say, listen, Charlie. This is Chief Kennedy talking. Is there a woman there by the name of Rhodes? She was. . . . She did, eh? How long ago? . . . I see. . . . What's that? . . . She asked you to mind a package for her till she got back? *(All look at each other, startled.)* Where have you got it? . . . In the safe? . . . Say, listen, Charlie. Call headquarters right away and get a man over there. Give him that package, and tell him to bring it up to Baldpate Inn as quick as he can. Understand? . . . Never mind, you do as I tell you. And listen. Tell them to guard the garage and the depot, and put all strangers under arrest, men and women. . . . I know what I'm doing, Charlie. You take orders from me. And listen. Get the coroner on the 'phone and tell him to get up here to Baldpate Inn in a rush. This is a case for him. . . . Don't lose any time now. Keep your mouth shut and get busy. *(Hangs up receiver and comes to* C. *All come forward.)* She left the hotel a quarter of an hour ago. She put the package in the hotel safe before she went. *(He looks them all over. They stand staring at each other.)* Humph! Somebody kills a woman—the victim disappears and then comes back! That's pretty good stuff!

MAGEE. *(Aside to* MARY, R.C.) How do you account for this?

MARY. *(Aside to* MAGEE) She must have stolen the money from me as we were running down the mountain. *(Whistle is heard outside door. All turn and look toward door.)*

KENNEDY. They've got somebody! *(Rushes up to door and unlocks it.* COP *enters.* CHIEF *locks door.)* What is it?

COP. A woman.

KENNEDY. Shoot her in. *(Unlocks door, opens it, and closes it as* COP *exits.)* Here comes the bird, I guess, that tried to fly away with the coin. *(Opens the door as* MRS. RHODES *appears. She enters and watches* KENNEDY *as he locks door.)*

MRS. RHODES. *(Turns, takes in situation, then to* CHIEF) What is the meaning of this?

KENNEDY. *(Up near door)* That's what I'm trying to find out.

MRS. RHODES. *(Goes to* MARY, R.C.) Is there any trace of the money?

(MARY *turns from her without replying.* MRS. RHODES *then turns and looks at men, who all give her a contemptuous look.* KENNEDY *comes downstage* C., *standing back of her.)*

HAYDEN. *(Crosses to* L.C., *between* CARGAN *and* KENNEDY) Are you going to have these women searched, Chief?

SEVEN KEYS TO BALDPATE 91

KENNEDY. *(Down L. of* MRS. RHODES*)* Maybe it won't be necessary. *(Looks intently at* MRS. RHODES *over her L. shoulder.)* We'll wait until we see what's in the package she left at the Commercial House. (MRS. RHODES *starts, regains her composure, then seeing all watching her, she turns and makes a dash for the door.* CHIEF *speaks as he follows her up.* HAYDEN *crosses back to L.)* No, you don't! Nobody leaves here until this whole thing has been cleared up and I find out who killed that woman.

MRS. RHODES. *(Turns, startled)* Killed a woman! *(Over to* CARGAN.*)* What does he mean? (CARGAN *turns from her without speaking. She goes to* MARY.*)*

MARY. *(To* MRS. RHODES*)* You stole the money from me, didn't you? (MRS. RHODES *goes to* CARGAN *without replying to* MARY.*)*

CARGAN. *(Looks* MRS. RHODES *straight in the eye)* I'll never trust another woman as long as I live!

PETERS. (R.) They're no good—they never were.

KENNEDY. *(To* PETERS*)* Shut up! *(Comes to* MRS. RHODES *at C.)* Well, what have you got to say, Missus?

MRS. RHODES. *(After a pause)* Yes, I did steal the money.

(MARY *looks at* MAGEE; *others look at* MRS. RHODES.*)*

MRS. RHODES. *(Over to* CARGAN, L.*)* But I did it for you, Jim Cargan. I knew that if the story was ever made public you would be a ruined man. I knew the package of money was the evidence that would convict you. I intended to return it to Mr. Hayden and try to kill off the bribe and save you from disgrace. I did all this because I thought you cared, and what is my reward? You stand there ready to turn against me—to condemn me. Very well, now I'll turn! *(Turns to* KENNEDY.*)* Officer, these men have bargained to cheat the city of Reuton. I demand their arrest on the charge of conspiracy!

HAYDEN. It's a lie!

MAGEE. It's the truth, Chief, the absolute truth. This young lady and I will testify against these men and prove them guilty of conspiracy and murder.

MRS. RHODES. Murder!

KENNEDY. What have you got to say to this, Mr. Cargan?

CARGAN. Nothing at all—I'm through. *(Sits at table* L. BLAND *goes upstage, then crosses to above table* L.*)*

MAX. So am I. I can't stand this any longer; I'm going mad! *(Goes to* CHIEF. PETERS *takes chair* MAX *vacates. During following speech* MAGEE *takes* MARY *up* R.*)* I want you to know the real truth. 'Twas I who killed that woman upstairs. I shot her down like a dog. I know that I haven't got a chance, but I don't want to be sent to the chair. I'll confess, I'll tell the truth, I'll turn State's evidence, anything—but, for God's sake, don't let them kill me! *(Kneels at* KENNEDY's *feet.)*

KENNEDY. *(To* MAX*)* Get up. *(*MAX *rises.* CHIEF *takes handcuffs from his pocket.)* Come on. You'll have to wear these, young fellow. *(Puts handcuffs on* MAX. MRS. RHODES *goes to foot of stairs.)*

BLAND. *(Throwing up hands)* There we go!

HAYDEN. *(To* CARGAN*)* What are we going to do, Cargan?

CARGAN. No less than ten years, I'm afraid.

KENNEDY. *(To* MAX*)* Go on, get over there. *(Pushes* MAX *over* R., *then goes upstage* R. *and down in circle.* MAX *takes* PETERS' *chair.)*

SEVEN KEYS TO BALDPATE 93

Mrs. Rhodes. *(Goes to* Mary, r.c.*)* Can you ever forgive me?
Mary. *(Giving* Mrs. Rhodes *her hand)* I didn't understand—I do now. *(Both go to foot of stairs, crossing in front of* Chief.*)*
Kennedy. *(Down to* Magee, r.c.*)* And you came here to write a book, eh?
Magee. That was the original idea.
Kennedy. You know, I don't know yet whether you people are kidding me or not. (All *turn toward door as police whistle is heard.)* They've got somebody. *(Rushes up to door and unlocks it. Cop enters. He closes door.)* Well, what now?
Cop. *(Hands package to* Chief*)* A package brought to you by the police messenger. He says it's from the Commercial House. *(All start.)*
Kennedy. Tell the messenger to hurry back and to tell the coroner to hurry up. *(Opens door.* Cop *exits.* Chief *locks door and comes downstage a bit, a sickly smile on his face.)* Say, before I open this thing, I want to tell you something. If this turns out to be a bunch of cigar coupons, I'm going to smash somebody, sure. I won't stand to be strung, even if I am a small town cop. *(Opens package and sees bills.)* Great Scott, it's the real thing! How much did you say was here?
Magee. Two hundred thousand dollars.
Hayden. *(Goes to* Kennedy, c.*)* I'll take that money, please; it belongs to me.
Cargan. *(Goes to* Kennedy c.*)* No, it doesn't; it belongs to me.
Magee. You hold that money, Chief; it's the only real evidence of bribery we've got.
Kennedy. Go away! (Hayden *goes upstage;* Cargan *goes* r. *of chair at table;* Magee *goes* c.*)* You needn't tell me what to do; I know my business. (Hayden *crosses to* l. *of table.* Kennedy *puts money in his pocket and goes to 'phone. As he does*

94   SEVEN KEYS TO BALDPATE

so, all on stage back up and watch him. In 'phone) Hello! Get me 13, Central. *(Wait.)* Hello! Is that you, Jane? . . . This is the Chief. I want to talk to my wife. *(Wait.)* Hello! Hello! Betty? . . . Listen, Betty; get this clear. Get some things together and get the children ready and take that five o'clock train to New York. . . . Never mind now, listen. When you get there, look up the railroads, and get on the first and quickest train that goes to Montreal. . . . Montreal. I'll be there waiting for you Thursday morning. . . . Don't ask a lot of questions; do as I tell you. . . . What are we going to do there? We're going to live there. . . . Montreal. . . . I don't know. *(Turns to* MAGEE.*)* How the hell do you spell Montreal? *(No one replies.)* Listen; go to Canada—any part of it. I'll find you. . . . What? . . . Never mind the furniture; we're going to live in a palace. . . . Canada, that's all. . . . You do as I tell you. *(Gets up from 'phone and goes* c.*, looking at the money. As he sees everyone staring at him, he puts it in his pocket.)*

MAGEE. What do you think you're going to do?

KENNEDY. You heard me, didn't you? I'm going to Canada.

PETERS. Canada! I hope to God you freeze to death!

MAGEE. You mean you're going to steal that money?

KENNEDY. Why shouldn't I steal it from a gang of crooks like this? It's one chance in a lifetime to get this much money. You don't suppose I'm going to pass it up when I've got it right here in my kick, do you? Not me! I'm going to have one hell of a time for the rest of my life and send my two boys to college!

BLAND. *(Over to* KENNEDY*)* Do you imagine we're going to stand by and let you get away with it?

SEVEN KEYS TO BALDPATE 95

KENNEDY. *(Whips out his gun and backs upstage a trifle. All but* BLAND *and* MAGEE *back away from him.)* That's just what you're going to do, and I'm going to have my men keep you here all night until I get a damn good start!

(BLAND *knocks the gun from the* CHIEF's *hand.* MAGEE *grabs his arms and pins them behind him.* BLAND *gets a hold on his legs. Women scream and run halfway upstairs.)*

MAGEE. I've got him! Get that money!
PETERS. *(Rushes toward* KENNEDY, *yelling)* I'll get it! I'll get it!
KENNEDY. *(Yelling from the time he is grabbed)* Let me go, do you hear! Let me go!
PETERS. *(Grabs money from* CHIEF's *pocket)* I've got it!
CARGAN. *(Starts for* PETERS) Give me that money!
HAYDEN. *(Starts for* CARGAN *and grabs him by the arm when the latter is* C.) No, you don't, Cargan; that's my money.
MAGEE. Don't let them get it, Peters!
PETERS. Let them try to get it! (BLAND *and* MAGEE *release the* CHIEF.) Now let me see you get it! *(Throws money in fire, laughing viciously. All stare into fire, watching the money burn.)* Watch the rotten stuff burn!
MAGEE. *(Comes down* C.) What have you done!
BLAND. He's burned the money!
CARGAN. A fortune!
HAYDEN. Good God!
KENNEDY. I'll have my men here and shoot you down like a pack of hounds! *(Starts up* C. *as two pistol shots are heard outside.* BLAND *goes* L., *near women.* MAGEE *goes up* R.; CARGAN *to table* L. MAX *goes* R. KENNEDY *goes up toward door.)*

MAGEE. What's that? *(All turn and stare toward door.)*
MAX. *(Looks up on balcony and yells)* Look, look! *(All look up on balcony as he points to* MYRA, *who is walking from room to room* R.*)*
PETERS. A ghost! A real ghost!

(MARY *screams and grabs* MAGEE; MRS. RHODES *screams and grabs* CARGAN; HAYDEN *crouches* L.; BLAND *jumps behind desk;* MAX *huddles up in chair near fire;* PETERS *is on his knees.)*

MAX. Take her away! I didn't mean to kill her! Take her away!
KENNEDY. *(Yells)* Let me out of this place! It's a graveyard! *(Starts for door. Door flies open and the* OWNER *enters. All stare at him.)*
HAYDEN. *(After a pause)* The seventh key!
BLAND. The seventh key!

(MARY *runs to* MRS. RHODES, R. MAGEE *goes up center.)*

KENNEDY. *(To* OWNER*)* Who are you?
OWNER. *(Standing at door)* I'm the owner of Baldpate Inn. Two policemen refused to allow me to pass, and I shot them dead.

(MAGEE *comes down to* C.*)*

ALL. What!
MAGEE. This isn't true! It can't be true! I'm a raving maniac!
OWNER. *(Comes downstage to* R. *of* MAGEE*)* I just arrived, Billy. I motored from New York. I expected to find you alone. *(Looks around at people, circles up* R. *and back to* C.*)* Who are these people? How did they get in here? Have they dis-

turbed you in your work? How are you getting on with the story?

MAGEE. How am I getting on? Great heavens! man, to what sort of a place did you send me? Nothing but crooks, murderers, ghosts, pistol shots, policemen, and dead people walking about the halls. Hundreds of thousands of dollars, and keys and keys and keys! You win—I lose. Twenty-four hours! Why, I couldn't write a book in twenty-four years in a place like this! My God, what a night this has been!

(OWNER *starts laughing, then all join in, laughing and talking ad lib.* MAGEE *stands looking at them in utter amazement.*)

OWNER. I'm not going to hold you to the wager, Billy. I just want you to know it isn't real.

MAGEE. What isn't real?

MRS. RHODES. *(Steps toward* MAGEE, *smiling)* I'm not a real widow. *(Crosses to foot of stairs.* MARY *comes down* C. *The* OWNER *goes up to desk, laughing.)*

CARGAN. *(Comes to* MAGEE*)* I'm not a real politician. *(Goes upstage.)*

KENNEDY. *(Down to* MAGEE*)* I'm not a real policeman. *(Backs upstage.)*

PETERS. *(Comes downstage to* MAGEE*)* This isn't real hair. *(Takes off wig and goes upstage* R.*)*

HAYDEN. *(Goes to* MAGEE C.*)* These are not real whiskers. *(Takes off whiskers and goes upstage* L.*)*

BLAND. That wasn't real money that was burned. *(Goes upstage* R.*)*

MAX. *(Over to* MAGEE C.*)* These are not real handcuffs—see? *(Breaks handcuffs and goes upstage* R.*)*

MYRA. *(Appears on balcony* R.*)* I'm not a real dead one. *(Hearty laugh from all.)*

MAGEE. *(To* MARY, *after looking around in amazement. Goes to her,* L.C.*)* Are you real?

(OWNER *comes downstage to* C.*)*

MARY. Not a real newspaper reporter.

MAGEE. I mean a real girl.

MARY. *(Smiles)* That's for you to say.

MAGEE. *(Turns to* OWNER*)* Well, for heaven's sake, don't keep me in the dark. Explain, tell me what it all means.

OWNER. It means, old boy, that I wanted to prove to you how perfectly improbable and terrible those awful stories you've been writing would seem if such things really and truly happened. I left New York an hour ahead of you to-day. I got to Reuton at nine o'clock to-night; went directly to the Empire Theatre; told the manager of our bet; framed the whole plan; engaged the entire stock company; hired half a dozen autos; shot over to Asquewan after the performance, and we arrived at the top of the mountain at exactly twelve o'clock. Since then you know what's happened. I've been watching the proceedings from the outside, and if it were not for the fact that I'm nearly frozen stiff, I'd call it a wonderful night. *(All laugh heartily.)*

MAGEE. You did this to me?

OWNER. *(Laughs)* You're not mad, are you? Of course, if you want to go through with the bet, why——

MAGEE. No, thanks; the bet's off. I've had enough of Baldpate. Me for the Commercial House until the train is ready to start. *(Over to* MARY, L.C.*)* Is your real name Mary? *(She nods affirmatively.)* Well, Mary, the shots in the night, the chases after fortunes, and all the rest of the melo-

SEVEN KEYS TO BALDPATE

drama may be all wrong, but will you help me prove to this man that there is really such a thing as love at first sight? *(All show interest.)*
MARY. How can I do that?
MAGEE. Don't you know?
MARY. Well, you don't want me to say it, do you?
MAGEE. *(Whispers in her ear—she nods affirmation)* Now remember your promise, Mary. *(Hearty laugh from all as he kisses her.)*

(Lights go out and black drop falls for about thirty seconds. End of Act II.)

EPILOGUE

(Curtain goes up again. Fire is out and lock replaced on door. The stage is bare. Typewriter is heard clicking from room R. on balcony. The clock strikes twelve. ELIJAH QUIMBY is seen outside waving a lantern as he did in the first act. MRS. QUIMBY appears, etc. Same business, except that instead of unlocking the door, he raps on it. When MAGEE enters from room R. and gets to C. of balcony, QUIMBY raps again. MAGEE comes out on balcony with hat and coat on, and carrying the suit and typewriter case and a manuscript under his arm. He stops on stairs, and as he hears QUIMBY'S rap he comes down the stairs, puts the cases on the table L. and then goes up to door and unlocks it.)

MAGEE. *(As he opens door)* Come right in, folks. You're right on time, I see. *(Closes door and locks it.)*
QUIMBY. *(Comes down R.C.)* We've been out there ten minutes waiting for the clock to strike.
MRS. QUIMBY. *(Comes down R.C.)* Lord, I didn't think we'd find you alive!

MAGEE. *(Comes down* C.*)* The only difference between me and a real live one is that I'm tired, hungry and half dead.

QUIMBY. (L. *of* MRS. QUIMBY) How'd you come out?

MRS. QUIMBY. Did you finish your book?

MAGEE. *(Handing* MRS. QUIMBY *the manuscript)* Allow me.

QUIMBY. What do you think of that, Mother?

MRS. QUIMBY. Lord! Wrote all that in twenty-four hours!

MAGEE. Just made it. Finished work a couple of minutes ago.

QUIMBY. Were you disturbed at all?

MAGEE. Never heard a sound. *(Sits at table* L.*)*

MRS. QUIMBY. No ghosts?

MAGEE. Nary a ghost, Mrs. Quimby, except those concealed in the manuscript. *(Rises.)* How about the Asquewan hotels? I'd like to get a bath and a bite to eat before I take that train.

QUIMBY. There's the Commercial House.

MAGEE. The Commercial House! That's strange! I guessed the name.

MRS. QUIMBY. How?

MAGEE. I've got it in the story.

MRS. QUIMBY. *(Aside to* QUIMBY*)* What's he mean, Lije?

QUIMBY. *(Aside)* Darned if I know. *(To* MAGEE*)* The Missus has got a fine breakfast waiting for you up at our house.

MRS. QUIMBY. And a nice feather bed for you to take a nap in. The train don't go till five.

QUIMBY. And the drummers all say the hotel's rotten.

MAGEE. Lord, I'm tired! *(Sits at table* L.*)* Me for the breakfast and the feather bed. Some wild and woolly scenes have been enacted in this room since you left last night, Mrs. Quimby.

MRS. QUIMBY. What happened?
MAGEE. Nothing, really—just in the story.
MRS. QUIMBY. What's he mean, Lije?
QUIMBY. How do I know? *(Telephone rings.* QUIMBYS *start and look toward it.)*
MAGEE. *(Goes to 'phone, stops buzzer, and then goes* L.*)* There's Bentley—he's pretty near on time.
QUIMBY. Will I talk to him?
MAGEE. Of course. That's the idea, isn't it?
QUIMBY. *(Goes to 'phone—*MRS. QUIMBY *stands* C., *watching him)* Hello! hello! Mr. Bentley. . . . Yes, sir, I've got it right here, sir. Two minutes ago, sir. . . . I'll have to find that out. Wait a minute. *(To* MAGEE*)* What's the name of the story?
MAGEE. It's typewritten on the cover.
MRS. QUIMBY. *(Holds up script and reads by light of lantern)* "Seven Keys to Baldpate."
QUIMBY. *(In 'phone)* "Seven Keys to Baldpate." *(To* MAGEE*)* He's laughin'. *(Pause, then to* MAGEE*)* He says there's only one. *(In 'phone)* Hello! . . . What, sir? . . . Wait, I'll see. *(To* MAGEE*)* You want to talk to him?
MAGEE. No. Yes, just a minute. *(Goes to 'phone.* QUIMBYS *goes* R.C. *and stand listening.)* Hello! hello! Hal. I'm going to collect that five thousand from you, old pal. . . . Yes, some title, isn't it? And, say, some story. Wild, terrible, horrible melodrama as usual, the kind of stuff you always roast me about. Treated as a joke, however, this time. And say, Hal, listen; I've got you in the story. . . . Yes, really. . . . Oh, I didn't mention your name or anything. . . . And, say, I'm in the story, too. . . . Oh, I'm the hero. . . . Say, Hal, this thing's going to sell over a million copies. . . . The what? The critics? *(Laughs.)* I don't care a

darn about the critics. This is the stuff the public wants. . . . Yes, I'll meet you at the Forty-fourth street club at two-thirty to-morrow. *(Ad lib. as the curtain falls.)*

SLOW CURTAIN

SET PROPERTIES

(All Wicker Furniture.)

1. *Hotel counter up* R.C. *to* R.
2. *Large practical safe back of counter,* R. *of* C.
3. *Register, ledger, etc., inside safe.*
4. *Practical telephone switchboard* R. *at end of counter.*
5. *White sheet thrown over switchboard.*
6. *Letter and key boxes on scene back of counter.*
7. *Large armchair front of fireplace,* R.
8. *Wood-box with fire wood and three asbestos logs above fireplace,* R.
9. *Low stool above wood-box,* R.
10. *Rack, with poker, tongs and shovel, below fireplace.*
11. *Gas firelog, andirons and fender.*
12. *Two chairs, stacked, front of counter,* R.C.
13. *Armchair* R. *of center door.*
14. *Armchair and plain chair, stacked,* L. *of* C. *door.*
15. *Round table, with chair on top of it, down* L.C.
16. *Two chairs, stacked, above and to* L. *of table.*
17. *Armchair below swinging doors,* L.2.
18. *Dust cloth on stair banister* L.
19. *Practical bracket lamp on pillar above fireplace,* R.
20. *Same above swinging doors,* L.2.
21. *Coils of fire hose, axes and extinguishers on scene* R. *and* L. *on balcony.*
22. *Keys in doors leading off balcony.*
23. *Practical typewriting machine off* R.3E. *above fireplace.*

24. *Small table and two plain chairs in room off balcony* R.
25. *Manuscript of story in room off balcony* R.
26. *Plain chair and bed linen in room off balcony* L.
27. *Wind machine off stage up* L.C.
28. *Blower off stage* L. *of* C., *near center door.*
29. *Bell chime off stage up* L.
30. *Table for hand props off stage* L.

HAND PROPERTIES

Seven keys for center door for characters.
One suitcase; one typewriting case; copy of agreement (long hand) and watch for MAGEE.
One sure-fire revolver (under counter) for MAGEE.
One package of money and one revolver for BLAND.
One revolver for CARGAN.
One sure-fire revolver for MAX.
One police whistle and one pair break-away handcuffs for KENNEDY.
Pipe and tobacco; box of matches; flask of whiskey; key to linen closet; telegram; watch and lantern for QUIMBY.
Lantern and sheet for PETERS.
Package of money in envelope for First Officer.
Police whistle; two small sure-fire revolvers and blank cartridges for property man.

ELECTRIC CALCIUM PLOT REQUIREMENTS

Four blue floods, two R. *and two* L., *on ceiling from fly gallery.*
One blue Olivette on back drop from L.4E.
One red Olivette in fireplace, R.2E.

ELECTRIC LIGHT PLOT REQUIREMENTS

One row white footlights on dimmer.

One white strip light on ceiling in one—on dimmer.
Six bracket lights on pillars on dimmer, switch L. of
C. door.
One white bunch light on transparency—back drop
L.5E.
One single incandescent lamp in room on balcony up
R.—Out.
One single red incandescent lamp in fireplace.
One single red incandescent lamp in fireplace flashed
when money burns.

Working Plot, Act I, Scene I

At Rise:
    Blue floods on ceiling—stand through.
    Blue Olivette on back drop—stand through.
    White bunch light on transparency, back drop.
Cues:
1. When Quimby lights lamp—foots slightly up with lamp.
3. When Quimby puts log on fire, red glow from incandescent lamp in fireplace.
4. "Old John H. Seclusion himself" (Magee), brackets and footlights full up together.
5. Magee snaps off brackets, foots down about one-half.

Working Light Plot, Act I, Scene II

At Rise:
    Floods, blue Olivette on drop and foots same as at fall.
    Bunch lights back of drop—Out.
    Red box light in fireplace.
Cues:
1. Magee snaps on brackets after ladies' entrance. Foots full up with brackets.

SEVEN KEYS TO BALDPATE

2. MAGEE *snaps off brackets before* PETERS' *entrance. Foots one-half down with brackets.*
3. MAGEE *snaps on brackets after* MYRA'S *entrance. Foots full up with brackets.*
4. MAGEE *snaps off brackets after ladies go upstairs. Foots one-half down with brackets.*
5. MAGEE *snaps on brackets after* MAGEE *shoots.* Foots full up with brackets.

N.B.—*Lights stand until curtain.*

ACT II

AT RISE:
Lights same as at fall of curtain.
CUES:
1. CARGAN *snaps off brackets after* MYRA *is shot. Foots down one-half with brackets.*
2. KENNEDY *snaps on brackets after his entrance. Foots up full with brackets.*
3. MAGEE *kisses* MARY. *All lights out.*

N.B.—*As soon as curtain is closed, put on white ceiling strip and put on foots one-third up. Put on floods and box light and strip on back drop. At cue from stage manager, put out ceiling strip—stands through.*

SEVEN KEYS TO BALDPATE

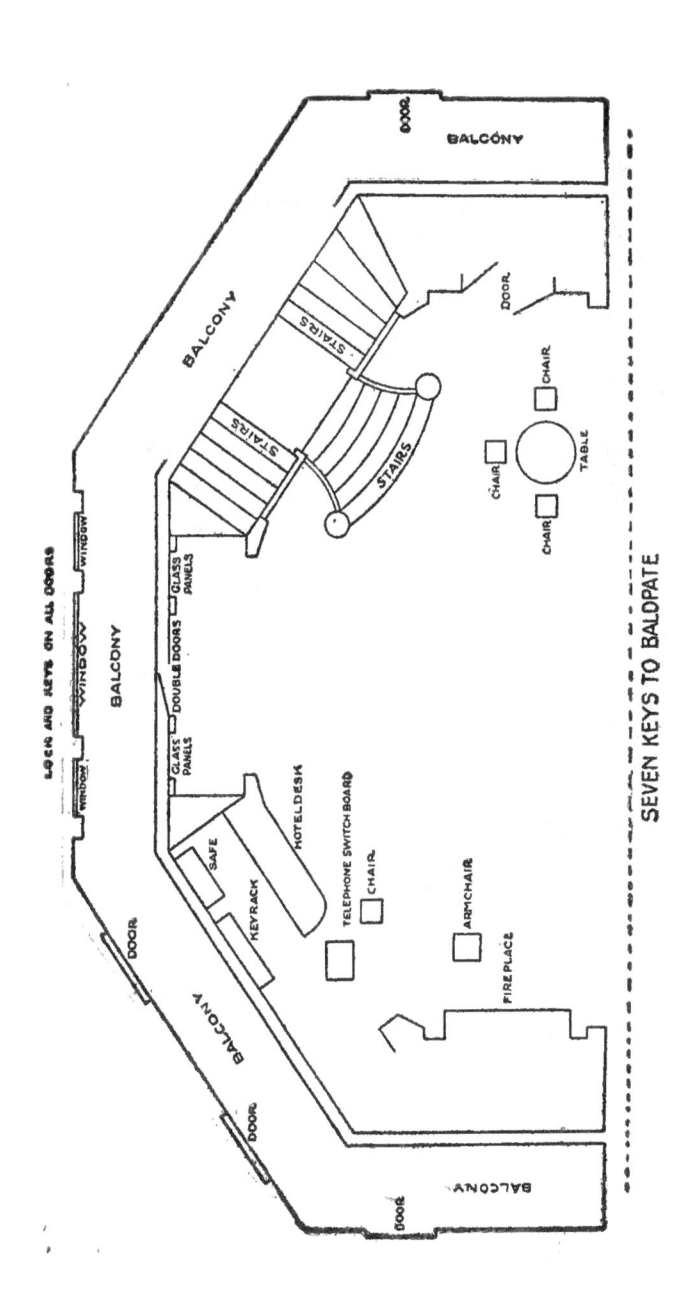

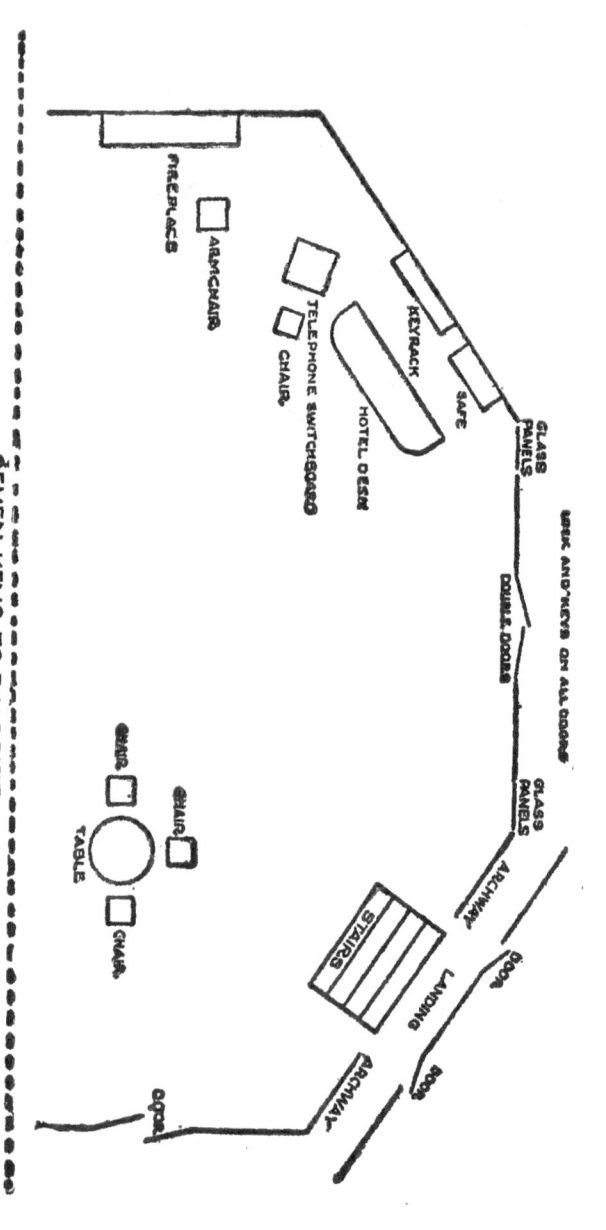

SEVEN KEYS TO BALDPATE
SIMPLIFIED STAGE SETTING

NOTE: Where the stage is found to be too low to admit of a balcony across the back of the stage, two doors, side by side, can be placed opposite the landing at the top of the stairs, which need only be three or four steps. If more cannot be arranged. If this is done the stairs should go up through an archway, and enough space allowed R. and L. at the top of the stairs for a character to be concealed from those on the stage.

See diagram

Ph.
CP.
at w.
LVH.
7611.

ted in the USA
A information can be obtained
w.ICGtesting.com
050255161023
6LV00006B/1044